PRAISE FOR *RECLAIM*

"*Reclaim* is an essential life skills guide, and a must-read for anyone enmeshed in an unhealthy relationship, whether at work or at home. Lisa Wilson's 3-part transformational process guides readers to recognize where and how they are giving away their power and energy; to restore their inner relationship with themselves, and to make life choices that are consistent with their own unique values, wisdom and desires."

—Sharon Strauss, Ph.D., psychologist

"Relationships are the final frontier. I believe their purpose is to guide us back to ourselves; to deeper understanding, and deeper love. But in order to use relationships to learn, grow and expand, you must first RECLAIM the truth—that the love you're seeking comes from within. In *Reclaim*, Lisa Wilson provides an inspiring perspective on what self-love looks like on a moment-to-moment basis, both through the lens of her own personal experiences and those of her clients. This book will be a guide to many on the journey back home to themselves."

—Joe Hawley, former NFL player,
founder of the Härt Collective

"Finally, a book that guides us to realize that the most important relationship we can invest our energy in is the one we have with ourselves. This is the path to finally shifting negative patterns and creating powerful, positive relationships with others. *Reclaim* helps you first to see and understand why you have made the choices you've made; second, to know that who you have been doesn't need to define who you now are; and third, gives you powerful (and simple) ways to shift and reclaim your personal power."

—Kristen Howe,
founder, Go Big Coach

"*Reclaim* is a gift to the world. Lisa Wilson is a brilliant example of a woman who was born into an abusive family in order to recognize her soul's purpose. By refusing to play the victim one more minute, she pulled herself out from under a goliath challenge of narcissistic exploitation from every direction.

Lisa's commitment to honoring the Divine Spark within drove her to explore and ultimately master the arts of self-love, confidence, healthy boundaries and mindfulness. Through this book, as well as her coaching practice, speaking engagements and personal growth workshops, she now excels in her sacred service of guiding others to do the same."

—Suzanna Kennedy,
women's empowerment coach

Reclaim

The Surprising Gift of Toxic Relationships

Reclaim
The Surprising Gift of Toxic Relationships

LISA J WILSON

Editors: Danielle Dorman—dldorman@san.rr.com; Nina Shoroplova—ninashoroplova.ca
Cover Designer: Cassie Clouser—thebrandmythologist.com
Book Interior and E-book Designer: Amit Dey—amitdey2528@gmail.com
Photo credits: Carl Studna—carlstudna.com
Publishing Consultant: Geoff Affleck, AuthorPreneur Publishing Inc.—geoffaffleck.com

ISBN: 979-8-9869391-0-0 (paperback)
ISBN: 979-8-9869391-1-7 (eBook)
ISBN: 979-8-9869391-2-4 (audiobook)

Library of Congress Number: 2022918393

OCC019000 BODY, MIND & SPIRIT / Inspiration & Personal Growth
PSY036000 PSYCHOLOGY / Mental Health
SEL023000 SELF-HELP / Personal Growth / Self-Esteem

For Sam,

May this book be your map if you
ever question or doubt yourself.

I love you.

FOREWORD
by Renee Marcou

*R*eclaim: *The Surprising Gift of Toxic Relationships* is a must-read for everyone who struggles at setting and maintaining personal boundaries – at work, with friends or family, and especially within intimate partnerships. Whether you are currently stuck in the confusion and overwhelm of trying to extricate yourself from a toxic relationship, or still feeling the effects of early childhood patterns that are subtly undermining your power today, Lisa Wilson guides you out of victimhood and into the full ownership of your intrinsic value. In just a couple of pages, in fact, you will start to feel whole and complete again, and so much more mindful of your energy and those you permit to access to it from this point forward.

Lisa and I met over a decade ago, as co-participants in a coaching certification course. From the moment we connected, I was drawn to her honesty and intuitive healing abilities. At the time, I was still reeling from the abrupt ending of a romantic relationship that left me deeply shaken, and once again face-to-face with the same core patterns and beliefs I'd developed in childhood.

Like so many girls in our culture, I was raised to be polite and agreeable, and taught by the well-meaning adults around me that this was the best way to guarantee acceptance, approval, and success in life. And as a result, as a young adult I learned the hard way about the steep costs of people-pleasing and the importance of setting personal boundaries. Like many women, I spent many years of my life ignoring my own inner voice for the sake of making other people happy. Suffice it to say that I found myself nodding along with these pages as if Lisa wrote this book specifically for me.

What this book helped me to distinguish in a very powerful way is that "fawning" is *not* an aspect of feminine power, but a trauma response that robs us of our creative energy and keeps us repeating self-sabotaging patterns at work, with our friends, and most certainly in the realm of relationships. I now understand at a whole new level that saying 'no' to someone else is saying 'yes' to myself, and that not only is it okay to love myself first, listen to my intuition, and move in the direction of the desires that are dear to my heart, but I absolutely must put these internal pieces in place before I can truly be of value to anyone else.

The steps laid out so clearly and beautifully throughout this book helped me to break a long-standing pattern of giving my power away and allowing my energies to be used by those whose intentions are at cross purposes to my own. I am walking away from these chapters feeling more empowered, intuitive, and deeply connected to my value.

Reclaim delivers the promise of its title. As you move through each of the book's three healing milestones, you will finally understand the motivations of those who seek to nourish themselves with your life force. You'll be guided to unpack the emotions and energies still lingering in your psychic field as a result of those experiences, and you'll gain the tools to align your life with the inner and outer boundaries that uphold your love for yourself. Lisa provides a safe and sacred space for this healing journey. In a style that is both radically honest and encouraging, she will help you move out of guilt and shame and into a life of empowerment and sovereignty.

Renee Marcou
CEO of Marcou & Co
award-winning international singer

CONTENTS

INTRODUCTION

This book was written for everyone who has ever been, is now, or may in the future find themselves in an emotionally abusive relationship, whether that relationship is in the context of an intimate partnership, a business setting, a spiritual community, or a family environment.

The principles and practices you will learn here are imperative for long-term physical, emotional, and spiritual wellbeing, and for creating healthy, interdependent relationships. They will not only provide a reliable means for extricating yourself from unhealthy dynamics in every relationship, but will show you how to become more aware of and responsible for the energy you are sending out into the world, because it is this energy that determines the quality of the experiences you draw to yourself.

In other words, in addition to providing a cure when you realize you're already in an unhealthy relationship, the information you'll receive from these pages will act as a preventative against ever entering into another one.

Being in an unhealthy relationship is an emotional roller-coaster ride that can trigger a wide range of feelings and experiences, one of the most universal being a nagging sense that you have somehow become disconnected from your own true north. Even if you previously defined yourself as a person of high self-confidence and discernment, when embroiled in an emotionally abusive or unhealthy relationship, your self-esteem plummets and you may experience intense self-doubt.

You might feel unseen, unheard, invalidated, and at times, as though you are going crazy. You may find it difficult to stand up for yourself or to speak out when your needs are not being met—or you may be great at speaking up for yourself, but find that your requests repeatedly go unmet. You probably feel as though you are being manipulated, deceived, or that your boundaries are being crossed, but may not be able to put your finger on any specific transgression. And even worse, you may spend hours replaying past situations in your head, trying to pinpoint where you went wrong, how you are to blame, and/or in what ways you could have more effectively contorted yourself in order to restore the peace.

The terms "unhealthy," "toxic," and "emotionally abusive" relationships, used throughout this book, neither refer to any particular psychological label nor to a diagnosis found in the DSM-5, the standard classification of mental disorders used by mental health professionals in the United States. If a healthy relationship consists of two strong and whole individuals interacting with one another without sacrificing themselves or compromising their values, then by definition a toxic relationship is one that is marked by compromise, dependency, manipulation, and powerlessness.

I define a relationship as toxic when either party consistently experiences any of the following:

- You feel powerless, confused, disconnected, or lost.
- You compromise or martyr yourself—your values, your time, your outside interests—for the sake of the other person's approval or happiness.
- You are unable to successfully communicate your needs, preferences, and desires.
- You are unable to establish or maintain personal or professional boundaries.
- You say yes when you want to say no.
- You feel discounted, taken advantage of, or used.
- You feel alienated from things that really matter to you, and out of alignment with your authentic self.
- You spend an inordinate amount of time fixated on the other person's feelings, experiences, and needs—to the detriment of your own.
- Your relationship with this person is driven by fear or scarcity, rather than by love and genuine desire.
- You repeatedly have feelings such as, "This isn't right," "This isn't good for me," or "I'd be better off without this person."

If even one of the sentiments described above resonates with you, it is my promise that you will receive tremendous value from this book. This is a bold claim, and it's one I can make with absolute certainty, because I know all the pitfalls along the road you've been on. I have personally navigated the path through emotional abuse many times in my life and have guided myself and countless others back to much safer and saner terrain. And above all else, I know the security, happiness, and freedom that await you on the other side.

Over the course of my life, I have had up-close and personal experiences with individuals who displayed all types and variations of emotional abuse. I was raised in a physically and emotionally abusive family, in which my parents, my grandparents, and my siblings all exhibited signs of narcissistic personality disorder. At the age of nine, I escaped the clutches of a predatory serial killer. In my late teens and early twenties, I attracted friends and co-workers whom I allowed to abuse me in all the same ways my family members had. And later, as a fully grown adult, I found myself in relationship after relationship with emotionally abusive or narcissistic men. My fear of abandonment drove me time and time again to abandon my own intuition, in a desperate attempt to contort myself to fulfill the ever-changing whims of whoever I was with at the time. With each encounter I was left drenched in guilt, shame, and regret for not standing up for myself and for once again giving my power away.

From a spiritual perspective, I can now see that the first half of my life was Divinely designed to provide me with a precise set of experiences that would set me firmly upon a ten-year journey toward self-love and self-healing. Sharing with others the wisdom I gained along this journey has since become my life's passion and purpose.

Whether I'm working with clients in the capacity of a law of attraction coach, neuro-linguistic programming practitioner, breathwork facilitator, certified hypnotherapist, or Reiki master, my intention is always the same:

To support those who find themselves embroiled in any type of dysfunctional or toxic relationship to develop the skills to reclaim a foundation of self-empowerment and self-love. These relationships might be at home, in the workplace, or even within the spiritual community where they turn for sustenance and a higher perspective.

This is the inner foundation we must strengthen, for a solid connection with ourselves is essential both for avoiding unhealthy situations in the first place, and for extricating ourselves from any we may find ourselves in.

At the time of this writing, I have guided hundreds of women and men through the transformative process of reclaiming their personal power, restoring their physical, emotional and psychic energies, re-establishing their values and boundaries, and becoming spiritually centered in their own lives. What I have borne witness to time and time again as a result of this work, within myself and with these courageous men and women—many of whom generously share their stories on these pages—is that our encounters with emotionally abusive people *always* come bearing a gift.

There is no situation, however dark, that does not bring with it a powerful opportunity to claim more of our light. Each event and relationship—even the most trying and painful—can be repurposed as an essential building block to becoming the versions of ourselves we truly want to be. We draw experiences like these into our lives for the precise purpose of becoming aware of all the cracks in our love for ourselves, so that we can set about the life-altering task of reclaiming that self-love.

It is to these individuals with whom I have co-created the most unsettling and toxic relationships that I feel the greatest gratitude. These experiences taught me how to navigate the winding terrain of claiming my autonomy, and of coming to know myself as a powerful, spiritual being. The individuals who pushed my boundaries the most taught me the paramount importance of listening to and trusting the ever-present voice of my own inner guidance, and ultimately set me upon the path of powerfully recreating my life—and my relationships—according to my own values and desires.

I share this because it is imperative that you know that whatever your situation, there *is* a path back to wholeness, and it is my promise to you that your experience, however dark or difficult, has neither been by accident or for naught, because there is great personal power waiting for you on the other side.

As you will learn, those we are in relationship with who act predatorily, who lack empathy, or who seem to demand the lion's share of our time and attention, provide an incredibly powerful mirror for us. And what is reflected back to us through our relationships with them are all the places within ourselves where we are not standing firmly in our truth and where we have relinquished our right to self-empowerment.

Whenever you're embroiled in any kind of dysfunctional relationship, it's as though your very center of gravity has been displaced. The sun of your own self-awareness—the vital energy that nourishes and sustains life and growth on the magnificent planet called You—gets redirected, and over time, your primary focus centers around another person over whom you eventually come to realize you have absolutely no control.

You have likely already discovered that no amount of energy, attention, validation, or self-sacrifice will ever be sufficient to transform someone, who is themselves emotionally imbalanced, into the whole, attentive, compassionate, and empathic person you desire them to be. In fact, the more you try to elicit the desired behavior from another person, the more trapped and powerless you feel.

This realization, this acceptance of things you cannot change, is the launching-off point of this book, because believe me when I tell you there is no use in squandering one more ounce of your precious life force trying to make yourself into what anyone else needs you to be. You can breathe a little deeper now, knowing that the work we'll do together on these pages will be focused entirely upon *you*. It will help you to distinguish the aspects of yourself that you *can* change—and perhaps deeply desire to change—and to separate these from the events of the past or the actions of others that you truly have no business accepting responsibility for.

This book guides you to the understanding that you—and no one else—hold the key to your own security, happiness, and sense of lovability. Once you discover this, you can stop pushing against what isn't working in any relationship and simply go where the freedom is. True freedom lies in knowing that by virtue of how, when, and on whom you direct the power of your attention, you can generate any experience within yourself that you desire, independent of the people and circumstances around you.

This book will not sugarcoat the truth for the purpose of helping you to temporarily feel better, nor will it provide you with strategies to tolerate an intolerable situation. In my experience, the self-help and spiritual community sometimes offers solutions that make us feel better in the moment, but don't lead us where we ultimately want to go. And while there is tremendous value in accepting others as they are and looking for what's right in each situation life brings us, our own wellbeing demands that we keep our eyes wide open and our feet securely grounded on the Earth.

This book will guide you along three consecutive milestones: Reveal, Restore, and Reclaim. Each of these will return you progressively to your own wellbeing and self-empowerment. After moving through each of these three sections, you will be able to trust yourself to evaluate, navigate, and liberate yourself from all manner of toxic people and situations. You'll be empowered to take greater responsibility for your own wellbeing, and you'll have the tools to masterfully direct your own energy in order to create the relationships—and the life—that you deserve and desire, deliberately and on purpose.

In part one, you'll gain the courage and the willingness to **reveal** to yourself the situations and relationships in which you are currently giving away an unhealthy amount of your energy or power. This section will distinguish the subtle, often unrecognizable characteristics of emotional abuse, which will help you not only to identify the toxic relationships in your life, but even more importantly, to identify the gaps in your own self-awareness that cause you to be attracted to and give your power away to these people.

Regardless of our particular backgrounds, all of us have been conditioned to look outside ourselves—to our families, relationships, careers, and other external circumstances—to find the inner sense of connection and security we crave. And when we come from the mindset that the happiness we seek exists in someone or something outside of ourselves, we become easy targets for emotional abuse. It's not easy to walk away from family, work situations, or romantic partnerships when we've been conditioned to believe that our security is tied to them, and someone who is emotionally unstable uses this understanding of our human conditioning to further throw us off balance.

In fact, in the same way that a seasoned hunter can instinctively track the path of his chosen animal and a savvy traffic cop has a sixth sense for catching lawbreakers, abusive or narcissistic individuals have an almost psychic ability to intuit our weak spots, trigger our emotional wounds, and locate the places within our psyche where a lack of confidence or self-awareness leaves us vulnerable to attack.

And so, the first part of this book leads you through a gentle but thorough self-assessment that will reveal the hidden places within your own psyche that leave you susceptible to toxic relationships. Where are you not honestly and clearly expressing your truth? To whom have you relinquished too much of your energy or your power? What messages has your intuition been trying to deliver that you have previously ignored? How is the life you are now living out of integrity with your deepest values and desires?

Once you've revealed the cracks in your energy field that make you an energetic match to abuse, you can begin the process of reclaiming and redirecting that energy back into yourself. Awareness is the first essential step to making any lasting change in our lives.

Part two guides you through simple yet powerful daily practices and inquiries, all designed to help you **restore** your relationship with yourself, repair your nervous system, and re-establish the lines of communication with your higher self and intuition. In this section, I'll teach you how to remain in tune with and in balance with your own energy field so you can receive the messages of your intuition while they're still a soft whisper rather than a desperate scream.

Developing trust in our intuition is key, because if we pay attention to our intuition and act on it accordingly, we will never fragment ourselves again. We will never allow any intruder inside our proverbial home, because our own internal alarm will sound the moment that person enters our sphere. And this time, because we are self-aware and willing to be responsible for upholding our own wellbeing, we're able to appropriately respond. Once we're back in tune with our emotional guidance system, using our inner truth to navigate our choices, a whole new realm of possibilities becomes available to us.

When we can trust ourselves to navigate the wide variety of relationships in our lives with no fear of losing ourselves in them, then we are truly free. This freedom is born from knowing that the most crucial choice we make in any moment is in how we view any particular person or situation, and consistently making the choice to view every experience as an opportunity for greater self-mastery and self-love.

In part two, I break down each and every component of what it actually means to love yourself; not in theory, but as a daily and even moment-by-moment awareness. The notion of self-love is thrown around so frequently that it's become a cliché, but to fully embrace it means we must restore within ourselves all the skills of awareness that make self-love possible. These include self-trust, self-respect, self-acceptance, personal integrity, and self-empowerment. It is in this, the largest section of the book, that you will learn the fundamentals of emotional, spiritual, and psychic wellbeing that will guard, support, and empower you in each and every aspect of your life.

Part three—**Reclaim**—will guide you through the most transformational shift in perception that any human being can make: from seeing ourselves as the victims of the experiences we've had, to understanding ourselves as the powerful co-creators of them. It's been said that we learn more from one year of pain than from ten years of comfort. This is because emotionally abusive relationships—once we understand how to process and assimilate them—always come bearing invaluable spiritual gifts.

So many of us who have chosen to be born at this unprecedented time in history have come in with a powerful intention to finally understand our true nature as Divine beings. And along with this quest for self-knowledge, our souls are orchestrating the very experiences that cause us to lose touch with who we really are. This is by Divine design, for in our disconnection from our authentic selves, our desire to return home is intensified. Yes, other people may have transgressed our boundaries and infiltrated those places in our psyches where we were not yet aware. But ultimately, it is our job, as the guardians of our own souls, to restore and then reclaim our physical, emotional, mental, financial, and spiritual wellbeing.

This section will lead you through the transformative steps to fully integrate the events of your past, first by accepting responsibility for creating your life experiences, and then by acknowledging the wisdom that each relationship came forth to teach you. I'll introduce you to a powerful process of reclaiming the parts of yourself that you have ignored, disowned, or given away, and identifying the core values that will support you in honoring these aspects of yourself going forward. You'll understand how and why fracturing off parts of yourself was actually an essential survival strategy, and you'll gain the tools to lovingly invite these valuable parts of yourself out of hiding and back into the light where you can benefit from the gifts they hold.

Once we receive the wisdom that is hidden within our emotional wounds, we liberate the energy that once held us in repetitive cycles of abuse. When our former emotional triggers are neutralized, they no longer hold any power over our experience and we're free to infuse our lives with a new frequency of energy and populate them with those who resonate in alignment with that higher frequency.

No matter what your situation—whether you are currently involved in an unhealthy relationship; you have noticed your tendency to attract a certain type of person into your life and desire to change that; or you are seeking greater self-knowledge so as to become more emotionally whole, aware, and resourceful—this book will equip you with the tools to restore your connection with your own inner guidance, to establish boundaries that support your physical, emotional, financial, and spiritual wellbeing, and to live the powerfully, self-actualized life you were born to create.

PART I

REVEAL

CHAPTER I

THE COVERT NATURE OF EMOTIONAL ABUSE

Tom met Rhonda just a few days after his divorce was finalized—an emotionally draining experience that had dragged on for over two years. The first thing Tom noticed was that Rhonda was nothing at all like his ex-wife. While both women were beautiful, Rhonda was downright sexy, and there was something wild and unpredictable about her that captivated Tom from the start.

In the beginning of their relationship, Rhonda was incredibly attentive and interested in Tom—a savvy businessman who ran a multimillion dollar business he'd started from scratch with just fifty dollars to his name. Unlike in his marriage, Tom felt seen and respected by Rhonda, who often sought him out for both personal and professional advice.

Within the first month of dating, Rhonda introduced Tom to her four-year-old daughter, and his attachment to the two grew quickly. Feeling compassion for Rhonda as a single mom trying to make a living for herself and her young child, Tom loved to spoil them by taking them horseback riding, to theme parks, and on lavish vacations.

Soon Rhonda began to hint that she was ready to take their relationship to the next level, making it clear that she was looking to get married and start a family of their own together. Tom didn't feel ready for this, having just come out of a twenty-year marriage, but considered it nonetheless. Rhonda was young and adventurous, and life with her was so full and exciting that he rarely thought about his hum-drum marriage or the pain that followed its dissolution. Besides, he had always wanted a family and liked the idea of adopting Rhonda's daughter and becoming the father she had never had.

When Rhonda began struggling to manage the various aspects of her fledgling business, Tom wanted to alleviate her stress, and offered to invest a sizable sum of money in her production company. Rhonda was traveling quite extensively to film a documentary and Tom often accompanied her. On the outside, they looked like the perfect couple. Soon Tom became fully invested in Rhonda and announced he was ready to take their relationship to the next level.

Around the same time that Tom began to genuinely lean into the possibility of marrying Rhonda, her behavior began to change. Whereas in the beginning she had been almost hyper-sexual and up for anything, she now began pulling back. Before traveling together, she would say things like, "I'm looking forward to our trip, but just so you know, I am not going to be intimate with you while

4

we're away." And then, for no apparent reason, she'd change her mind and aggressively seduce him. In the afterglow of their intimacy, Rhonda would make seemingly casual observations: Tom's teeth were crooked; his hair would look better if he grew it longer; and the clincher, she wasn't sure she wanted to be with someone who was ten years older than her. And while these flaws were never presented as serious objections or deal breakers, Tom registered them all the same. He had always felt confident about his looks, yet now found himself obsessing about how he could improve his appearance for Rhonda's sake. When the two argued, Rhonda's derogatory comments would escalate, and she told Tom on numerous occasions that she was not sexually attracted to him. This crushed Tom, of course, but not for long. Their make-up ritual always included passionate sex, which Rhonda enthusiastically initiated.

Tom grew more and more confused and was having trouble reconciling the disparity between Rhonda's words and actions. One minute she would gush about how much she loved him and wanted to spend the rest of her life with him, and the next minute she would crush him by bringing up what she now referred to as "the age thing." Once, in a flash of self-awareness, Tom confronted Rhonda about her contradictory behaviors, saying he didn't understand how someone who supposedly loved him could say such hurtful things. To this, Rhonda burst out crying and said, "How could you ever question my love for you? I have never, *ever* questioned your love for me!"

By this time, Rhonda was intricately involved in every aspect of Tom's life, but now, instead of being an understanding friend and intent listener, she expressed doubt and displeasure about nearly everything, from Tom's daily routine to his choice of friends. In an attempt to keep the peace, Tom gave up his passion for hiking and as time went on he spent less and less time with his friends. Eventually, Tom's confidence began to waver. On one hand, he had grown extremely reliant on Rhonda's attention; but on the other, he felt his own sense of autonomy slipping away. Truly lost, he began to question himself.

By the time we began our coaching work together, Tom was physically, emotionally, and financially enmeshed with both Rhonda and her daughter; he felt anxious a good deal of the time; and he had broken contact with everyone in his life who had cautioned him that he might be jumping too quickly into a new relationship. He told me that Rhonda was like his kryptonite, and also that he had come to feel simultaneously weaker and more dependent on her over time.

Rhonda had presented herself to Tom as a classic damsel in distress. She deliberately elicited the part of him that longed to be the hero, knowing that he wanted nothing more than to come to her aid and improve hers and her daughter's lives. But the more he gave, the more she asked of him, and any time he would pull back or request reciprocity, the more volatile and emotionally abusive she became.

Rhonda's tactics offer a perfect case in point. Because while it's true that emotional abuse can occur in the form of overt hostility, yelling, bullying, and demeaning behavior, in the vast majority of cases it is subtle, hidden, and covert. Her passive-aggressive verbal abuse, withholding of affection and sex, and gaslighting by feigning helplessness and innocence are much more insidious.

Even when emotional abuse is flagrant and obvious, it can still be incredibly difficult to prove or even recognize within a relationship. A battered wife or husband can admit themselves to an emergency room with clear evidence of a broken bone or black eye, but someone who's been emotionally abused can't take a witness stand and produce the same type of definitive proof. Emotional abuse is subtle and sneaky. It often begins so gradually that it's imperceptible. If it comes as a sudden outburst, it may have us chalk it off as a one-off event. Often we don't know we're engaged in a toxic relationship until it's too late to make an easy escape.

The Tale of the Boiling Frog

If you've ever been in any type of unhealthy or abusive relationship, you've most likely experienced a "come-to-Jesus" moment in which you realized your life has taken on the characteristics of a very bad nightmare. *How did I get here?* you ask. *How did I let this person get so close? How did things become this out of control?* Enter the Tale of the Boiling Frog.

The Boiling Frog refers to a series of science experiments that were allegedly performed on frogs during the late nineteenth century. In one such experiment, researchers placed a live frog into a pot of boiling water, and noted that the frog jumped out immediately. In the next experiment, they placed a frog in tepid water and gradually increased the water temperature. The second frog—while just as capable as the first frog of jumping free—was boiled alive, because the temperature of the water inside the pot was increased by such small incremental degrees that the frog never noticed. Such is often the case with emotional abuse. The abuser's tactics—while almost always carried to an extreme at the end—may begin so innocuously that we don't recognize what's happening until it's too late.

At the beginning of any abusive relationship, there is a honeymoon phase that blinds us to the unhealthy individual's deeper motivations. We might be wooed by the person's apparent success, crazed with sexual attraction, or influenced by the opinions of others who perceive this person as a "great catch" or "the nicest person in the world."

In this chapter, we explore some of the most common forms of emotional abuse that are often impossible to identify at the beginning of a relationship. And they're hard to identify for a very pointed reason: Those who seek power and control over others have a skillful, almost psychic, capacity for understanding and manipulating human behavior. They instinctively sense other people's weak spots, and have no problem at all exploiting them. Almost from the start, we experience an overwhelming need to win their attention and approval ... and with that initial almost-imperceptible displacement of our personal power, we set the stage for a relationship that grows more and more out of balance.

In every case, those who are emotionally abusive are disconnected from their own inner resources and seek control over others as a way to regain their sense of power, control, validation, and/or worthiness. In the presence of such a person, we feel on edge. Uncertain. Unsafe. Emotionally, we can't seem to find solid ground, and we're not able to articulate quite why.

Because developing an awareness of any situation is the first necessary step toward changing it, what follows are some of the most common strategies that emotionally abusive individuals use when attempting to manipulate or coerce others. As you read these descriptions, I invite you to acknowledge how many times you've been on the receiving end of these tactics.

"Love Bombing," Also Known As Charm and Attentiveness

When you first meet someone who uses love-bombing as a seductive tactic, you're likely to think this person is a genuinely amazing guy or gal. They're attentive, sensitive, and may even reinforce your outlook on life by recounting experiences similar to your own. They seem charming, empathic, agreeable, interested. And ... perhaps ... a little too good to be true?

This person is likely to make gestures, offers, or invitations very early on in an attempt to advance the relationship—to the point that a little voice in your head may start to whisper, "Whoa, this is moving really fast." This aggressive approach is deliberate. By coming on strong and fast, the abuser attempts to knock you off balance in order to distract you from any doubts or disbelief that may be arising. In the beginning, at least, being the object of this person's attention can feel so warm and flattering that we overlook or ignore any red flags alerting us that something about them is "off," that they may be emotionally unstable, or they may not have our best interests at heart.

Think of Rhonda, who in the beginning listened intently to Tom; who told him repeatedly that she found him sexually desirable, and who hung on every piece of advice he offered her about how to grow her fledgling business. This was not because she was interested in authentically knowing him or becoming genuinely intimate with him, but because she instinctively sensed that Tom had what she needed—namely money, status, and connections.

In addition to listening for what Tom could give her, Rhonda was also reading intently between the lines. What kinds of things made him feel proud, and what experiences undermined his confidence? She spotted right away his compassion for single moms, correlating this sensitivity with stories he shared about growing up with a single mother. She noted how he had built his successful business from scratch, and how much he respected those brave enough to take the risk of becoming an entrepreneur. She also asked about his previous marriage, and read the pain in Tom's face when he told her it was void of affection and intimacy, and how this had undermined his confidence.

Emotionally abusive individuals listen to those around them not for the sake of developing true understanding or intimacy, but with the intention of personally benefitting from the information. They are cunning, manipulative, and calculated in their approach; they will spend the necessary time "grooming" their victims by showering them with attention, love, and affection. But once they have built us to the point that they're confident we've become dependent on their attention, their focus shifts entirely, and they then go to work on breaking us down.

Mixed Messages

When someone we're in relationship with sends us mixed messages—as Rhonda did with Tom—we often begin to question ourselves rather than ask the other to clarify their communication. For example, as soon as Rhonda knew Tom was enamored with her enough to consider marriage, she changed her strategy to drive the hook even deeper. Making very slight and well-timed statements about his age or his sexual prowess accomplished the goal of keeping him a little insecure and off-balance, not enough for him to react to in the beginning but enough to get under his skin and sow the first seeds of self-doubt.

What makes this tactic even more confusing and therefore difficult to detect is that an emotional abuser will deliberately trigger one of our deep emotional wounds while simultaneously positioning themselves as someone who can help us out of our pain. For example, an abusive or narcissistic mother might say to her young adult daughter who is starting out on a new relationship or business venture, "Remember, I'll always be here for you." The overt message is one of assistance and concern, but the underlying communication is "You'll never make it on your own" or "You need me."

11

By triggering our underlying self-doubts and insecurities, the emotional abuser gains access to the deepest, most hidden, and least understood realms of our psyches. When this breach occurs, we feel off center, out of control, confused and—strangely—even more dependent on this person's continued attention to bolster our security. It is this dependency that gives ego-centered individuals access to what they are really after—power, validation, and control.

Isolation

Healthy relationships involve each partner maintaining a separate identity, upholding their own value systems and preferences, and having a life independent of one another, at least some of the time. But emotional abuse works best in secrecy and in isolation, and for this reason, abusers often seek to isolate their prey from family and friends.

They may do this overtly, by directly finding fault with the people you hang out with or insisting that those closest to you are out to sabotage your relationship. Or, they might use more covert and manipulative attempts to isolate you from those you love. They may "forget" that you've made plans with friends and present you with non-refundable tickets to a show on the same night, or you might notice that they seem to always have a crisis and need your attention every time you make plans without them.

The isolation tactic is another way that insecure and unhealthy people may attempt to gain control over you: the fewer people who are around to witness this, to love, and to care about you, the easier that job is for them.

Erratic Behavior

Emotional abusers run hot and cold: one minute passionate and affectionate, the next minute icy and distant. Their ambivalence and erratic behavior further confuses us and leaves us in a state of high alert—often to the point that *we* end up feeling like the "crazy" one.

This psychological tactic, known as intermittent reinforcement, was observed in a series of famous studies conducted on lab mice in the 1950s by psychologist and social philosopher B. F. Skinner. The mice were introduced to a lever, which, when pressed, would occasionally dispense a large treat, occasionally a small treat, and most often would yield nothing at all. Unlike the mice that received the same treat every time, the mice whose rewards were random and unpredictable developed a type of obsessive-compulsive disorder. They pressed the lever compulsively, and became so obsessed with obtaining the reward that they neglected mating rituals and even sacrificed water and sleep.

Emotionally abusive individuals intentionally use erratic behavior to instill within us an intense desire and attachment that we experience very much like an addiction. Think of the abusive husband who brings the wife flowers the night after assaulting her, or the mother who initiates a grand gesture of love and support after giving her child the silent treatment for an unreasonable length of time.

I once spoke with the child of a coaching client, whose mother regularly flew into sudden fits of narcissistic rage. These episodes seemed to come out of nowhere, and the

young girl was unable to identify a pattern that would protect her from the storm. I asked her one day what it was
like to spend time with her mother. "It's like a tsunami,"
she said quietly. "Except that you never know when a
huge wave is going to come and hit you." It was a fitting
and tragic description. One minute Mom interacted with
her like a supportive, concerned parent and the next minute
the little girl was the target of her mother's rage.

This pattern of cruel treatment peppered with unpredictable bursts of affection create a type of cognitive dissonance
within us that leaves us in a state of confusion and constant
rumination. *Why did he do that? What did I do to trigger it*
(both the negative *and* the positive treatment)? *What can I
do to prevent her from acting this way in the future?*

Ultimately, because we can find no rhyme or reason behind their erratic behavior, we begin to question
ourselves.

Human beings crave predictability and will spend huge
amounts of energy in an attempt to find it. Intermittent
reinforcement conditions the victim of emotional abuse
to keep seeking out the "big rewards" they once received
from the abuser, even in the midst of their mistreatment.
It's not unlike an alcoholic or cocaine addict: always up
for another round, no matter how steep the cost or how
bad the last hangover was.

Gaslighting, Also Known As "Turning the Tables"

In order for an emotionally abusive person to grab a
foothold in your life, they must successfully distract
you from what's actually going on long enough that

you've grown attached to the relationship before you realize what's happening. As we've already seen, they accomplish this through love-bombing, by being erratic and unpredictable, by going from hot to cold and back again on a moment's notice, and by consistently shifting the focus from them back to you whenever you confront them or try to get them to take responsibility for their behavior.

Recall again the case of Rhonda, who would flip flop from being overtly sexual with Tom, then moments after making love would offer a harsh judgment about his age or his appearance. When Tom confronted her, pointing out that her behavior was not consistent with someone who loved him, she turned the tables and tearfully said, "How could you accuse me of not loving you!"

Once again, the victim's focus is diverted away from his or her own inner experience of what's actually happening to the abuser's rendition of what they would have us believe.

"How could you do this to me?" is a classic battle cry of the emotional abuser, by the way. With statements like these, they are turning the focus from themselves back onto you, causing you to question your own perceptions and making you feel bad for ever bringing the subject up. By intermittently switching from pain to pleasure, from withdrawal to loving admiration, they are able to hide the fact that they're constantly shifting blame onto you.

In light of these descriptions of emotionally abusive behavior, it's easy to see how we often confuse an abuser's attempts to control or disempower us as gestures of love.

The mother who convinces her child that he's weak in order to keep him dependent ... The friend who constantly unloads on you in order to elicit the compassion from you that he's incapable of giving himself ... The wife who champions her husband's success, not because she is genuinely proud of his work, but because it garners the admiration and envy of her friends ...

These behaviors are not gestures of love. They are strategic methods employed to fill the void of another person's pain and insecurity—at the cost of our energy, our equanimity, and even our physical and mental wellbeing.

Depending on which walk of life you happen to encounter them, emotional abusers may present in a variety of ways. In a workplace setting, they may play the victim or lay blame on others in order to excuse their poor performance. In a social context, they may don the role of misfit or rebel, always with a story to tell about the mistreatment they've suffered or how the world doesn't understand them. In romantic relationships or support groups, they may lure you in with their tragic tale of woe, subtly inviting you to become their hero—only to later proclaim that you have "changed their life" and they cannot live without you.

Whereas a physically abusive person may hit you over the head with one fatal blow, the emotional abuser is more likely to poison you every day for ten years ... death by a thousand cuts.

Now that we've revealed some of the tactics an emotionally unwell person may use to gain access to our energy, we're ready for the next level of this inquiry. Because in order to develop a healthy degree of immunity against those who would use us to bolster their own sense of self, we must understand the *internal* factors that make us susceptible to their ploys. To gain this understanding, which is so vital to reclaiming our own empowerment and emotional freedom, we must reveal the unique ways in which each of us was imprinted—or constellated—within our early families of origin.

CHAPTER 2

YOUR PSYCHE'S BACK DOOR

Imagine that you're the owner of a magnificent home that you very much want to enjoy, preserve, and protect. And so, determined to prevent undesirable people from accessing your precious sanctuary, you install a security camera that captures everything that's taking place in the front of your home. But simultaneously as you are keeping a watchful eye on your front yard, undesirable people are coming in through the back and silently stealing your belongings. You're not even aware this is happening, because they're accessing your home through an entrance you don't realize exists.

This "back door" is both literally and figuratively a blind spot. In vision, blind spots occur when photoreceptor cells on the optic disc are missing, making certain parts of our field of vision invisible to us. In psychological terms, a blind spot refers to any aspects of our personalities that are hidden from our conscious view. Your psyche's back door refers to the gaps that exist in your own self-awareness that prevent you from deliberately attending to the sanctuary that comprises your body, your mind, and your soul. Only when you become aware that these gaps exist—and do the inner work to close them—will you be in a position to truly defend, uphold, and advocate for your own wellbeing.

Our back door—or psychological blind spots—are formed as a result of the emotional wounds we accumulate over our lifetimes, ones we have not yet allowed ourselves to feel, release, and extract the wisdom from. We're blind to these places within us, because they represent the parts of ourselves we've ignored, repressed, or disregarded—either to fit in, to win the love of others, or to feel less insecure. And here it is vital to understand that it's only through these gaps in our own self-awareness that toxic individuals gain access to our personal energy reserves. This is because our attention becomes so drastically displaced on the other person's needs, opinions, and approval of us that it is no longer available to carry out its most essential and life-sustaining task: guarding our safety and attending to our wellbeing.

Our core wounds—and the fight, flight, freeze, or fawn survival responses that spring into action when those wounds are triggered—are what give emotionally abusive individuals unhealthy access to us. Remember, those who feel powerless and seek energy from others are experts at locating the parts of our psyches that are strong and well-developed, as well as the parts of us that feel weak and deeply unworthy. They can sense our lack of wholeness. They know which of our primary survival responses cuts closest to the bone. They know how to trigger our deepest weaknesses, and have an almost supernatural ability to validate us in the precise ways we were never validated within our families of origin. In other words, they activate our core wounds on purpose, then present themselves as someone who has the willingness or the power to help us heal them.

Ultimately, of course, each of us is responsible for illuminating and repairing the gaps in our awareness that cause us to keep falling into familiar patterns of emotional abuse. And to gain this understanding, we need to revisit, from an entirely new perspective, the dynamics that were at play in our families of origin.

Illuminating Your Psychological Blind Spots

For decades, psychologists have understood that what happens between conception and the age of two has a profound influence on the type of adult each one of us will ultimately become. The baby whose basic needs are met early on is imprinted with the knowledge that the world is generally a safe place. He or she will retain this sense for life, almost as an instinct. In contrast, babies who are neglected or abused, whether physically or emotionally, develop a hypersensitive survival response (fight, flight, freeze, or fawn) that makes it extremely difficult for them to regulate—or even acknowledge—their own feelings.

Secure early bonding is the difference between the baby who grows up to be a resilient, emotionally boundaried, and capable adult, and a baby who grows into a depressive or anxious adult who does not easily cope with life's ups and downs. One child has been constellated within her family of origin to see herself as whole and complete. The other—never having received a healthy sense of her intrinsic importance within her family—feels incomplete and somehow broken. She then begins a lifelong journey, searching outside of herself for that very important and primary validation that every human being needs.

Family Constellations Therapy was developed by German psychotherapist Bert Hellinger in the mid-1990s. This therapeutic model was based on Hellinger's assertion that the energy—both positive and negative—that characterizes our familial bonds has an impact on the degree of value we place upon ourselves and on what we later perceive to be acceptable and unacceptable treatment from others.

The word "constellate" has several different significant definitions that can help us to better understand the dynamics with which it occurs in a person's family of origin:

Constellate:

1. (*transitive*) To combine together or form a cluster, like stars in a constellation
2. (*transitive*) To fit or adorn as if with constellations
3. (*intransitive*) To shine with united radiance, or as one general light

In an ideal world, when a child is born, her parents shower her with the love of the entire universe. In their gaze, she receives the message that she is perfect, whole, and complete as she is. She is a beautiful, desired, important contribution to the family, and as such, her very presence makes the world a better place. She is an integral part of the family and the universe in which she was born; she is, in fact, the beloved center of that universe. She belongs. She is constellated, integrated, and celebrated within her family of origin.

Those of us who were fortunate enough to be healthily constellated—which is to say, if we were seen and heard, and our feelings, needs, and boundaries were respected and regarded—were imprinted with a very powerful message early on. In the presence of our parents' or caregivers' steady attention, we were taught not just to trust ourselves and to honor our own feelings, but we also learned that we can trust our caregivers to provide comfort and reassurance in times of need. And by extension, we can trust that the universe is a friendly, safe, and abundant place.

Healthily constellated children learn that their feelings matter, and that they have a right to speak out when something or someone doesn't feel right. They are sensitive to their intuition and are more willing to follow the dictates of their inner guidance, even when it goes against the status quo. In our healthy and ideal state, we are integrated, whole human beings with a feedback loop that connects all dimensions of our being—body, mind, emotions, and spirit.

Fractured Constellations

When we are not imprinted early on with this subtle yet powerful knowledge of our innate goodness; if we are not raised within the loving understanding that even in our imperfection we are perfect; if our own parents were not whole enough within themselves to validate our worthiness or to celebrate our belonging within the family, then we are not properly "constellated." As a result, vitally important parts of us become fragmented.

In the shamanic worldview, this fragmentation (or what the shamans call "soul loss") occurs as a result of a traumatic event or chronic stress. In the face of danger or trauma, the energy body fragments and parts of the soul withdraw, repressing deep into our psyches or trapped in the time and space of the wounding event.

The term "soul loss" may sound devastating or dramatic, but literally *everyone* who is alive has experienced it to some degree. In fact, this fragmentation can occur in response to something very slight. Even a startle can create a psychological fracture. For example, if a mother leaves her child unattended in a grocery store for just a brief moment, she is out of the child's sight. Realizing he can't find his mom, the child panics. Even benign-seeming events like these can create an imprint, leaving behind a tendency of reactivity that we carry into our adult relationships.

CHAPTER 3

SURVIVAL RESPONSES: FIGHT, FLIGHT, FREEZE, OR FAWN

Back in 1915, Walter Cannon, a professor and chair of the Department of Physiology at Harvard Medical School, coined the phrase "fight-or-flight response" to describe the instinctual and biological reactions that all animals experience in the face of a real or perceived danger. The surge of adrenaline through our bloodstream prepares us either to run for our lives or to go to battle to protect them. When our fight or flight response is activated, our pupils constrict, making our vision more acute. Our breathing and heart rate increase to better oxygenate our bodies. Blood is diverted from less essential functions like digestion and into the limbs to power our muscles. In an instant, this primitive response helps us decide whether fighting or fleeing will give us the better chance for survival.

Since Cannon's initial discoveries, psychologists have identified two additional primal responses to real or perceived threats. Our "freeze" response has been triggered when, faced with a threatening situation, we suddenly stop dead in our tracks, our minds go blank, and we feel unable to move or even think. Freezing can also manifest in less obvious ways: dissociating from the triggering event, escaping it through oversleeping, daydreaming, watching hours upon hours of TV, or using drugs, alcohol or food to numb our awareness of the threat.

Most recently, San Francisco-based psychotherapist Pete Walker introduced yet a fourth survival response to perceived danger: what he calls the "fawn" response. In his 2015 book, *Complex PTSD: From Surviving to Thriving: A Guide and Map for Recovering from Childhood Trauma*, Walker explains,

> *Fawn types seek safety by merging with the wishes, needs and demands of others. They act as if they unconsciously believe that the price of admission to any relationship is the forfeiture of all their needs, rights, preferences and boundaries. They are usually the children of at least one narcissistic parent who used contempt to press them into service, scaring and shaming them out of developing a healthy sense of self: an egoic locus of self-protection, self-care and self-compassion.*

Unlike those who rely on fight, flight, or freeze approaches to survival threats, the fawn assumes the role of the people-pleaser in order to attempt to manage a dangerous or potentially dangerous situation. In the fawn response, we perceive that our survival is dependent on our ability to read another's energy and anticipate their needs, and so we contort and adapt our own behavior so as not to provoke the unwanted treatment.

Note that the fawn survival response is very different from healthy empathy. With healthy empathy, we have the capacity to read a situation or feel into another person's experience without losing our sense of self or our ability to advocate for our own needs. But the fawn response displaces our sense of self and temporarily hijacks our ability to attend to or even acknowledge our own needs. We actually feel that our survival depends on effectively managing someone else's feelings and behaviors—which, of course, we are powerless to do.

Children who were imprinted with a fight, flight, freeze, or fawn response as a result of early childhood conditioning often do not speak out against the family system, even when they're being mistreated, out of fear that doing so would actually threaten their very survival.

Children Who Are Neither Seen Nor Heard

As young children, we are one hundred percent dependent on our primary caregivers. Without their willingness to feed, clothe, and shelter us, our physical survival would be at great risk. But in the absence of their love, recognition, and acceptance of us, our psychological survival suffers just as significantly.

Whether our childhood wounding takes place on a physical, emotional, or psychological level, we are compelled to hide it, minimize it, or justify why we deserved the mistreatment. To face the possibility that our caretakers are ill equipped to care for us, or worse— that they regard us as an energy source for meeting their unmet needs—is simply too painful for a child's psyche to bear. So, rather than feel the pain, we repress it. We decide that the abuse is our fault, and that if only we were prettier, smarter, better behaved, or fill-in-the-blank, we'd be deserving of the affection, recognition, and acceptance that every child needs to thrive.

In the same way we place a Band-Aid over a physical wound to keep it from getting reinjured, we create a false, more accommodating version of ourselves to cover over the parts of us that were judged, rejected, or—worse—never even seen at all. And the more we inhabit this false self for the sake of keeping the peace, the further disconnected we become from our authenticity, our intuition, and our power.

And so, we don't say "ouch," or, "please don't do that again," when we've been wounded, because we feel we can't risk the further loss of our caregivers' love. Instead, we become whoever we feel we need to become in order to ensure they will continue to provide for us. For example, if sensitivity was a trait condemned as weakness, you might have tried to change or hide this part of yourself, or felt such shame about it that you expressed it only when no one else was around. If self-sacrifice was viewed as a character strength, you may have worked hard to win the title of "Mommy's Helper" or "Daddy's Big Boy."

Based on our early experiences as children, we form all kinds of conclusions about who we need to be—and who we must *never* be—if we want to retain the love and vital support of those around us. So, even though we may have been deeply wounded by those who truly should have acted as our protectors, we cover the wound, too afraid to speak out even when our physical or psychological health is at risk.

Let's look at a real-life example of how this can play out.

After her mother abruptly left when Charlotte was three years old, everything that she associated with security, safety, and comfort vanished from her experience. She describes it as a vibrant, beautiful Technicolor movie suddenly turning to black and white. Charlotte's father was a busy professional, now faced with the challenge of raising two young children alone. Within months of meeting Leigh, a single mother of a fourteen-year-old son, Charlotte's father married Leigh and they combined their households.

Charlotte, now four, looked up to her new stepbrother, John. In her mind, she fashioned him as the older brother she'd always wanted: someone who would love her, watch over her, and protect her. After months of feeling nothing but despair and uncertainty, John's arrival in Charlotte's life brought a flicker of security on the horizon.

Whereas Charlotte had become used to spending long stretches of time alone, she was now the object of John's attention—lots of it. His interest in her made her feel important and special, and the fact that he often asked her to play together in a private fort he'd built in their backyard made her feel he regarded her as his equal.

Unfortunately, John was not interested in protecting Charlotte or in treating her as anything close to an equal. What started out as innocent-seeming games of Cops and Robbers gradually escalated into full-blown sexual abuse that continued for over two years. Charlotte's own intuition told her there was something very unhealthy about this relationship, but she desperately craved the attention their encounters provided. It was only after her body began manifesting undeniable signs of sexual abuse that she found the courage to take a stand against her perpetrator in such a way that he never laid a hand on her again.

While it could be argued that Charlotte was simply too young to recognize what was happening, this was not the case. Her intuition had begun sending signals about her wellbeing from the moment she and John first "played" together alone. The reason, I believe, that children like Charlotte fall prey where other children do not is due to the blind spots that exist, hidden, within their own psyches.

At four years old, Charlotte was too vulnerable to allow herself to fully feel the intense abandonment she experienced following her mother's abrupt departure from her life. Searching for someone or something to fill that void, she saw John not for who he actually was, but for who she wanted and needed him to be. She grew reliant on the attention he paid her, and—unwilling to risk the withdrawal of that attention—she ignored every impulse that arose within her to signal that something was very wrong. Like many little girls of that generation, Charlotte adopted a fawn survival response as a primitive way of coping with a very unhealthy family constellation.

Sickness Within the Family System

The families in which we are raised are living organisms, and each individual within our family culture has a profound influence on every other individual. When the family is led by healthy, functional parents who provide consistent attention to the children, each individual thrives, even when inevitable conflicts arise. But when one or more family members is emotionally unstable, his or her behavior sends a ripple effect throughout the entire family system that thwarts the healthy development of every other member. Depending on the specific dynamics, the psychological wounding can take many different forms and occurs in varying degrees of severity.

Let's look at another case in point.

Michelle was the youngest of three girls born to Wendy, an extremely self-absorbed and unstable single mother. Michelle's father had left the family shortly after Michelle's birth, disgusted that Wendy had once again failed to give him the son he had always wanted. But rather than devoting herself to her daughters' care, Wendy set out on a path to find herself a new husband. She went out nearly every night, leaving the girls with whichever babysitter happened to be available and bringing home a constant string of new boyfriends.

Susan, the middle sister, had been five years old when Michelle was born, and was jealous of Michelle from the beginning. Instinctively, Susan understood the limited amount of attention her mom was interested in devoting to being a mom. She resented any attention

31

that Wendy paid to Michelle, and began looking for the attention she desired in manipulative and deeply destructive ways.

On the surface, Susan positioned herself as Michelle's caregiver and protector. When Monica, the eldest daughter, left home for college when Michelle was just five, Wendy left much of Michelle's welfare in ten-year-old Susan's hands. Susan stayed home to babysit Michelle five nights a week so their mom had the freedom to go out.

Michelle idolized Susan and relied on her for almost everything, and for a short time, Michelle's admiration and dependence provided Susan with sufficient narcissistic fuel. But over time, Susan's need for attention, importance, and power grew, and she began manipulating Michelle in cruel and sadistic ways.

On one occasion when Michelle was still five, Susan chose a rare family get-together in the backyard to lead Michelle into a carefully planned trap. She told Michelle to walk to the fence where the neighbor boys were playing and say the words, "Fuck you." Michelle obediently did as big her sister asked, only to receive the shock of her mother dragging her inside the house by her hair and shoving a bar of soap in her mouth. On another occasion when Michelle was again in Susan's care, Susan told Michelle that a huge earthquake was predicted to strike their town at 2 a.m. Then, laughing, she proceeded to go out with her friends, leaving Michelle terrified and alone in the house until morning.

Incidents like this were commonplace throughout Michelle's childhood. Like most abusers, Susan instinctively knew that in a psychologically broken state, Michelle was more vulnerable and therefore easier to control. Susan would knowingly lead Michelle into danger—both to feel the rush of the power she had over her, and to then show up as the rescuer, thus deepening the younger girl's dependence on her.

Sometimes the wounds inflicted on us in childhood are intentional; many times they are not. Michelle's mother was not herself a balanced or resourceful-enough human being to provide Michelle with the care she needed or deserved. Nor was she attentive enough to Michelle's feelings to recognize her daughter Susan's manipulation tactics, or the ways in which Susan constantly violated Michelle's boundaries. Within her family of origin, Michelle was "constellated" and groomed to be someone who gave her power away at all costs. To keep the peace with her sister and mother, Michelle trained herself to submit in those moments when she most needed to speak her truth and set a solid boundary.

To this day, even after years of therapy, Michelle still finds it challenging to speak out when one of her boundaries has been crossed. This is a muscle that Michelle must continue to strengthen through awareness, loving kindness, and practice. It is the core wound that continues to play out for her over and over.

The Disowning of Our Personal Power

As we've seen, when we are unhealthily or incompletely constellated within our families, we are not imprinted with messages of wholeness, but with those of lack and insufficiency. We learn early on that our safety and security rests in the hands of our caregivers, and so—like Michelle and Charlotte—we abandon both our inner guidance and our personal agency for the sake of pleasing those whom we believe hold the power over our wellbeing.

We learn not to feel our feelings, not to express our needs, and not to speak out against mistreatment for the sake of attending to our caretakers' needs instead. The bond between parent and child is both literally and figuratively a lifeline. We focus as much energy as is required to keep that bond intact—even if it means tolerating abuse from other family members.

Over time, the most powerful and unique aspects of ourselves get buried deep within our unconsciousness— hidden from our awareness and therefore inaccessible to us. What we *do* begin to recognize as time goes on and we grow into teenagers and adults is that we seem to keep recreating intimate relationships, friendships, and work scenarios that remind us in some haunting way of the dynamics that were enacted in our families of origin.

If we conclude early on that it was some flaw in our character that caused our mistreatment, we will continue to attract people who mistreat us. If we decide that the reason we didn't receive the affection, recognition, or acceptance we deserved is because we are unlovable, we may pour love into other people to a fault, hoping that in our giving, we will finally be re-constellated into wholeness. And of course, an emotionally unhealthy person *does* seek to re-constellate us, but in ways that meet his or her needs, to the detriment of our own.

Despite the fact that we've disowned and disconnected from our emotional wounds, they do not cease to exist. In fact, these blind spots are responsible for leading us time and time again into unfulfilling or even predatory or dangerous interactions with others. This is because our emotional wounds carry energy that is magnetic in nature. Like powerful cellular transmissions, the parts of ourselves we have not yet uncovered and embraced call to us people and situations that puncture the wounds, reveal them, so that we can begin the journey of self-discovery and healing. Until they are healed, our wounds will continue to define who we are and what we believe we are worthy of. They dictate the quality of people and experiences we allow into our lives.

One of the greatest gifts that emotionally abusive individuals give us—and one which we'll explore in depth in the following chapter—is the opportunity to work out in real time the wounds that are still operating beneath the surface, influencing everything from our self-worth to our day-to-day choices. Most often, these patterns continue to replay over and over in our lives, until such a time that our deepest wound is punctured and we finally gain the courage to look inside.

Our awareness of self—of our ever-changing needs, feelings, and boundaries—holds the key to understanding our susceptibility to another person's negative intentions, and to developing the tools that can keep us psychologically immune to their attacks. This self-awareness is a 24/7 job. It requires that we first develop the sensitivity to recognize the internal messages our intuition is constantly sending, and next, we cultivate the determination to honor those signals. Ultimately, the value of this book does not lie in helping you to recognize those who, as a result of some deficiency within themselves, seek to use your energy to make themselves whole. The real value of this book is to help you recognize the gaps in your own self-awareness that leave you susceptible to such attacks.

A Self-Assessment

The following self-assessment will help to uncover the hidden places within your psyche that make you vulnerable to emotional abuse: Where are you not standing in your full empowerment? To whom have you given away too much of your energy and power? Which of your precious qualities were never "constellated" and celebrated within your family of origin? In what ways are you still looking for someone else to make you whole?

Place a check mark next to each statement that accurately describes you.

- I am sensitive to even subtle fluctuations of energy in the people around me.

- I find it difficult to maintain my mental focus or emotional equanimity when someone I love is upset.

- I have a tendency to give too much to the people in my life, and often don't realize until after the fact that I feel depleted.

- Gaining the acceptance and approval of other people is important to me.

- If someone I love is hurting, I feel compelled to drop everything in order to soothe or support them.

- In my family of origin, I rarely felt seen, respected, or understood.

- I tend to look for and assume the best in others, even if we've just met.

- It's difficult for me to ask for what I need.

- I often don't realize one of my personal values or boundaries has been crossed until after the fact.

- My first instinct is to avoid, rather than to initiate, confrontation.

- I frequently have experiences with other people that leave me feeling shameful, guilty, or powerless.

- I can usually tell when someone I love is upset.

- I grew up with the notion that selfishness is bad.

- There are parts of me that feel incomplete; I look to others to feel whole.

- When faced with a decision, I tend to value the opinions of the important people in my life over my own instincts or inner guidance.

- At work, it's easier to pick up others' slack, rather than cause trouble.

- In my relationships with others, I often feel as though I'm walking on eggshells.

- I don't react well when other people disapprove of me.

- My preferences are fluid; I'm fine when I'm going with the flow.

- In my personal relationships, I often feel as though I give more than I receive.

- When someone close to me acts in a way that opposes one of my core values, I am more likely to stew about it silently than to bring it up in a serious conversation.

If you placed a check mark next to no more than five of these statements, you most likely have a high degree of self-awareness and therefore a higher-than-average immunity to emotional abuse.

If you placed a check mark next to between five and ten of these statements, there are definitely aspects of your psyche you are not fully conscious of. The more light you bring to these blind spots, the more self-awareness you will gain.

If you placed a check mark next to ten or more of these statements, you have a strong tendency to displace your sense of self, your sense of value, and your personal power onto other people and circumstances. The tools and processes you will learn throughout this book will be of immeasurable value in helping you restore your sensitivity to your inner guidance, and your willingness to advocate for your own best interest.

Before we move into part two of this book, into the life-giving process of restoring your nervous system, reconnecting with your intuition, and rebalancing your energy field, it is vital that you understand one crucial fact:

Your susceptibility to emotional abuse has nothing to do with weakness or naivety. In fact, in the vast majority of cases, those who are targeted by emotionally unstable individuals are strong, successful people who enjoy healthy relationships in every other aspect of their lives.

What transpired as a result of your involvement with the abusive people in your life was not your fault. You didn't "deserve it." You are smart, capable, and stronger than you know. You were targeted not because you are weak, but because you have tremendous strength and value. You could even say it's a back-handed compliment if you've been the target of another's emotional abuse, for they only seek out those whom they perceive have something of value to give. You are about to awaken to the strength of your own power and to the depth of your value and gifts.

PART II

RESTORE

CHAPTER 4

TENDING TO YOUR INNER WORLD

I like to envision the healing process of restoration as taking place within a series of concentric circles. The innermost circle reflects our core vibration. This is the way we think and feel about ourselves and our lives, on a moment-by-moment basis, within the silent realm of our hearts and minds. Everything we manifest in our lives radiates outward from this central vibration: the lifestyle choices we make; the way we show up in our careers; and ultimately the degree of autonomy, self-regard, and personal empowerment we carry with us into our relationships with others.

Creating harmonious relationships with others only becomes possible when we are in a state of harmony within ourselves. When we're in tune with and responsive to our needs and desires, when we welcome our emotions for the valuable guidance they provide, when we're clear about our own personal boundaries and willing to uphold them, this inner harmony is reflected in all our outer actions. But when there is disharmony within us—if we've been denying rather than honoring our emotions; or if we're cut off from our deeper needs and desires; or if instead of practicing self-compassion we're beating ourselves up with shame or regret—then this chaotic energy ripples out into all our endeavors and interactions. And as you've no doubt discovered, the discord we experience internally has a way of swiftly attracting individuals and situations that are uniquely qualified to amplify our internal chaos. The only way to change the tide of this unhealthy dynamic is to restore the natural balance within ourselves. This is the inner work of restoration.

When you right the ship of your own inner world, when you lovingly attend to yourself first and foremost, and when you make it your priority to feel a little better today than you did yesterday, you gradually build momentum that will, with practice, begin to reverse the tide. And I can assure you that any attempt to shift something in your external life *must* begin with this inner work. No matter how much you may believe that it's possible to do this process in reverse—that is to first establish harmony with another person, hoping that this will restore your core vibration—it just doesn't work that way. Your outer world is a reflection of your inner world. And the dynamics that occur in your relationships with others reflect the quality of the relationship you have with yourself.

The solitary time in between relationships is vital. If we don't give ourselves an opportunity to turn inward, to pause, reflect on, and refresh the signal we're sending into the universe, the next relationship we attract will be unsatisfying in many of the same ways.

This is a time to rediscover yourself and to take a stand for what it is you truly desire—and don't desire—rather than saying yes to people and experiences that don't feed your soul. It's a time to value *being* over *doing*, introspection over interaction. It's a time to lean into the most precious relationship you will ever have with a human being—your relationship with yourself. To a large extent, conditions in the outer world have a way of working themselves out when you re-establish balance in your inner world.

Layers of Restoration

By now you have an understanding of the blind spots in your own psyche that can leave you vulnerable to unhealthy or abusive relationships. You understand that the unhealed wounds from your early upbringing carry an energetic frequency that is still active and alive, which attracts others who are fragmented in a similar or corresponding way. And hopefully you're beginning to realize that you are the only one who can repair the cracks in your energy field that make you an easy target for emotional abuse.

This is the perfect time to give yourself permission to disengage for a while, and to reorient your focus toward your innermost center. It's a time to declare that you are worthy of the luxury of being the primary beneficiary of your own time, attention, and energy. Many times without realizing it, we stay in relationships that don't serve us as a way of distracting ourselves from addressing the bigger changes that life is nudging us toward. Unhealthy relationships can offer the perfect cover (both an excuse and an alibi) for why we're unable to create the results we desire or bring our lives into alignment with a higher frequency.

Those of us who've been in toxic or abusive relationships understand how easy it can be to find familiarity in a chronic environment of tension and uncertainty. Oftentimes we stay, afraid to let go of the chaos for fear of what the silence may reveal. All of these fears I understand—both from personal experience and from having coached hundreds of clients through the process of restoration. And I am here to tell you with one hundred percent certainty that any fears of going within and of becoming intimate with yourself are but illusions.

Your natural state is one of resiliency and peace. Every aspect of your being is designed to return to equilibrium, regardless of how far out of balance it has become. Your emotions may be turbulent on the surface, but if you soften into them and grant them permission to be—if you allow them to move through you without judgment or resistance—you'll find that, like a wave, they will peak and then subside.

You may have spent the better part of a lifetime running from the most precious task any of us is assigned in this life: the task of taking extraordinary care of ourselves; of parenting ourselves with the same degree of intentionality and attention that we would extend to our own child. And when that child has been hurt, as you have, to take every step necessary to nurse that child back to health.

Getting back to a state of neutrality, to ground zero, is essential work. Yet it's a step that many of us on a spiritual path tend to skip. We've learned that our thoughts create, so we try to bounce as quickly as we can from despair back into a state of appreciation. And in so many cases, it's simply too big a jump. To borrow a common New Age catchphrase, we try to distract ourselves from the sight of an empty fuel gauge indicator by covering it with a smiley face sticker. We may feel relieved for the moment, but we haven't really solved the problem.

I certainly understand the value of reaching for a better-feeling thought or perspective, but too often these amount to little more than spiritual bypassing. We're using positive affirmations, visualizations, and other techniques to paint over an energy imbalance within us that desperately needs our loving restoration. And if we don't attend to this vital inner work, we'll continue to magnetize people, experiences, and situations that draw our attention to the work that's yet to be done.

The work of restoration unfolds in sequential layers, and here in part two, we'll gently and lovingly unpeel them all. The work begins with an intention to disconnect our energetic fields from the unhealthy relationships and situations that have manifested in our external lives, and to redirect our attention back to the rich, fertile field sphere of our inner world.

Getting to Ground Zero

Trying to create anew when we're in the midst of turmoil is a bit like trying to construct a house on a site cluttered with rubble from the previous structure. We first have to take the time to clear the ground, to repair the lines that bring needed water and electricity to the land. Then, from a state of clarity and connection, we can start building with no fear of sliding back. It's time now to assess the damage to the house that is your body, mind, and soul, and to lovingly put each broken piece back into place. I invite you to view this not as a chore but rather as a life-changing, trajectory-altering opportunity to rediscover who you are, identify what's truly important to you, and declare which of your heartfelt desires you now wish to bring to life.

Regardless of our present circumstance, the work of restoration is always beneficial. Like the nighttime that brings cooling relief to plants and animals, and the tide that recedes to gather strength before it rises again, restoration is a necessary part of our life cycle. It's the key to building resilience, to finding and maintaining emotional balance, and it always comes bearing with it the enormous gift of relief.

And so, this is a time to do the internal, restorative work that I call "cleaning up your side of the street." And although my ultimate desire is to give you the skills to create healthy, supportive relationships, at this stage of your healing journey I encourage you not to think about relationships at all. Simply focus on you, and on restoring your equilibrium and inner resiliency.

This is a time to rediscover who you are at your essence, and to then slowly begin introducing your authentic self to the world, in baby steps that feel good along the way. The work you're about to embark upon will support you in nurturing a solid and secure home base—literally and metaphorically—both in the physical home in which you live and in the heart of your spiritual center, which you bring with you everywhere you go. You're about to discover—or be reintroduced to—the foundational practices that will reliably lead you back to a state of inner alignment, regardless of the situation or walk of life you find yourself in.

You have tolerated a lot. You've put up with a lot of discomfort. To some extent, you were that proverbial frog in the pot troubled by the gnawing awareness that the water was slowly heating to a boil. And now, simply by virtue of picking up this book, you have begun orchestrating your own liberation. For even if you're still living or working with an unhealthy or emotionally abusive person, you're now seeking your own freedom.

This freedom, and all that it will make available, is my promise to you.

Before we dive into each of the restorative rituals and practices outlined here, I would be remiss not to begin with a word of caution: *If you have any reason to believe that your wellbeing or the wellbeing of a loved one is at risk, it is imperative that you reach out for whatever professional support you may need to extricate yourself from that dangerous situation.*

For the work of restoration to be effective, your immediate physical safety must be a given. In the same way you wouldn't turn to acupuncture or homeopathy to heal a broken leg, energy- and intuition-balancing practices will not keep you out of harm's way if your physical safety is in jeopardy. If you are, or fear that you are, in any immediate danger, please visit www.RadicallyAuthenticYou.com, where you will find a resource section offering a list of organizations and agencies that provide needed counseling and support. The restorative processes that are offered here are provided with the assurance that they can support your psychic and emotional health, but they are inadequate modalities if your physical wellbeing is at stake.

With that said, I also encourage you to take the steps that follow in the sequence they've been provided, literally like peeling an onion. What you'll discover is that this is a process of first emptying, then filling. Each layer of restoration creates the foundation of stability and equanimity that gives rise to the next.

You've summoned the courage to take this important first step. Now begins the work of restoring yourself back to a state of balance and peace.

CHAPTER 5

CREATING RESTORATIVE SPACE

R estoration requires time and intention, and also a safe
space that you can retreat to, to unplug and unwind.
However large or small a space you have to call your own,
this is the time to fully inhabit and sanctify that space.
Whether you live alone in your dwelling or share a home
with another, the first step in your restorative process is to
put some energy and intention into transforming it into a
place of simplicity and peace.

Begin this process by clearing any excess clutter from
your environment, removing anything that lowers your
mood or introduces sadness, confusion, or static into
your vibration. And if you don't presently feel strong or
clear enough to make a decision about what to keep or
discard, simply place any questionable items in boxes to
store out of sight and attend to later. Remove unwanted
or triggering photos or other memorabilia from your
sight. Straighten your dresser, desk, and countertops.
Disinfect surfaces, launder linens and curtains, and wash
windows.

Once your home is clear and clean, you can begin filling it with things that bring in light, purify the vibration, and reflect the essence of who you are. Light candles and burn sage. Place healing crystals where they'll reflect and amplify natural light. Use essential oils shown to reduce stress, enhance mood, and raise the frequency of the human body: lavender, frankincense, and sandalwood.

You may want to place uplifting images or fresh flowers in locations where you'll see them often, or create and dedicate a small altar or meditation space for reading, journaling, and integrating all that you're about to uncover. Buy yourself a journal and pen to express feelings and insights and make note of anything within you that's asking to be acknowledged. Fill your space with high-frequency music such as Gregorian or Sanskrit chants, known for thousands of years to increase personal vibration and promote self-healing. And if ancient chanting isn't your thing, listen to whatever type of music settles you, or gets your energy moving – depending on what you need in the moment.

Allowing Blocked Emotions to Flow and Be Released

Emotion is simply energy in motion, and when not allowed to flow freely, this energy can get blocked within us, obstructing our ability both to perceive and respond to situations with objectivity. Built-up emotional energy takes a toll on both our physical wellbeing and our mental clarity. For these reasons, releasing it is often a really good place to start anytime you're feeling out of sorts.

To get your energy moving, go for a brisk walk, or put on some angry music and move your body. Scream into a pillow or buy a whiffle bat and beat the crap out of one! Allowing yourself a period of angry catharsis is of tremendous value prior to settling your energy down. It's an act of self-love to allow yourself to simply be where you are. Whatever emotion you're feeling, give yourself permission to name it, to claim it, and to own it. You first have to honor where you are before you can change things. The idea is not to linger in unpleasant emotions for days on end, but to really feel the emotions so you can let them go. Aim for creating a little more room within yourself—physically, mentally, and psychically. Give yourself permission to take up as much space as you need and move your body in whatever ways bring you a sense of relief.

Deliberate use of your breath is an effective way of releasing emotional energy, even when your body remains at rest, because your breath is a conduit between your physical self and the more subtle aspects of your being. Whenever you feel yourself moving even slightly off center, your breath is a go-to, regardless of the type of energy imbalance you're experiencing. To release anger, inhale forcibly and exhale with a loud sound. To soothe anxiety, breathe in slowly and deeply to a count of four and exhale slowly to the same count.

Journaling is another helpful way to mobilize and release stored emotions. Simply put pen to page or fingers to keyboard, and free write anything that comes to mind. The less you think about or try to censor what you're writing, the more effective this process will be. Your goal is not to come to any conclusions or even to make logical sense. Just use the journaling as a means for externalizing anything you've been internalizing. What is revealed when you later read your outpouring is often illuminating.

Basically, anything that spurs your physical, mental, and emotional energy into motion is a beneficial practice for releasing stored emotional energy, especially when this is your guiding intention while performing the action.

You can also use visualization to enhance your experience of stored energy leaving your body and mind. Whatever method you choose to release pent-up negative energy, visualize yourself standing in a shower and feeling the water washing away excess energy, as well as any patterns of thought that aren't serving you. If there is a particular frequency within the color spectrum that feels especially attractive or healing, imagine bathing yourself in this frequency of light and allowing it to gravitate to anyplace in your system in need of balance.

Unwinding Your Nervous System

As you already know from personal experience, anytime you're caught up in a fight-flight-freeze-fawn survival state, you have very little access to the higher realms of consciousness where wisdom, insight, and broader perspectives abound. In survival mode—whether real or perceived—our physical, emotional, and spiritual energies are chaotic and unorganized. The infinite resources of source energy are as available as always, but when we're in fight-or-flight mode, we flail about like the spinning beach ball on a frozen computer, unable to connect to the universal web that's there to soothe, support, and guide us. The fight-or-flight state triggers within us a cascade of stress hormones and other physiological responses that diminish our ability to respond resourcefully or mindfully to the situation at hand, putting us quite literally into a tailspin.

To make matters worse, those who seek to manipulate or control us are often really good at triggering our fight-or-flight response. Whether consciously or unconsciously, they've learned that it's easier to sway others in the direction of their choosing when we're off balance to begin with.

What's called for in moments like these is an intentional unwinding of our nervous system; we need to talk ourselves off the ledge of the fight-or-flight mode and back into a state of rest and repair. Because unless you're actually hunting your next meal or running from a tiger who sees you as his, there is very little use in engaging when your nervous system is on high alert. It's much wiser—not to mention more efficient in the long run—to take some time to ground your energy and unwind your nervous system. Make this your first order of business anytime you feel yourself entering a tailspin, and when it does come time to formulate a response, you'll find you have access to a much higher range of choices than you had access to while in survival mode.

There are many healing rituals and traditions that can help you to reset your nervous system when you find yourself wound a bit too tight. I've discovered that each one of us needs to experiment a bit in order to find the modalities that work best for us. Personally, I have been on a journey of healing and transformation for over twenty years. In my quest to master energy healing, I've studied everything from Shamanism and Soul Retrieval to rewiring outdated programs and limited beliefs. I'm a certified hypnotherapist, Reiki Master and Teacher, and Unity Bubble Breathwork facilitator, among other things. What I can tell you is that these days, the rituals I turn to for soothing my nervous system and getting to the other side of any challenging experience are pretty simple. I love going for an early morning walk in nature, followed by soaking in a hot salt bath while listening to bilateral beats, which have successfully been used to relieve everything from anxiety and stress to PTSD and insomnia.

Bilateral stimulation works by triggering electrical activity in different parts of the brain at the same time, which encourages better communication between the two sides of the brain. This inter-hemisphere communication could hold a key, both to helping us regulate nervous system functions and to processing emotion more efficiently. Himalayan salt baths are thought to help purify and rejuvenate the personal energy field or aura by releasing blockages in the subtle body and thereby encouraging the release of emotions. This combination of healing modalities has become so habitual for me that I almost always experience a shift in consciousness after just a few minutes.

The most important thing to remember is that this, like many things, is an intuitive journey. There is no magic pill and no one right process. I encourage you to try many different methods until you find those that feel right for you.

Once your fight-or-flight response has been quieted and you've successfully soothed any chaotic energy patterns within your body and mind, you'll again be able to take in the big picture of a situation before deciding how—or if—you want to engage with it.

When you feel rested and ready for something new, consider taking on a creative project that feeds your soul. Paint, draw, write, design ... Do anything that gets you into your creative mind, as this is a powerful doorway to draw a new frequency of energy into your life. Tend a small (or large) garden. Make something for someone you love. Fill a medicine bag with little things that have meaning to you, things that have supported your journey of self-discovery. Take a class that you have always wanted to take. Indulge in learning something new. Cut out inspiring, life-enhancing words and images from magazines and paste them onto a poster board. Dig out an old picture of yourself from a happier or more connected time in your life and place it in plain view.

Very often, unhealthy relationships involve a gradual—sometimes imperceptible—relinquishing of our personal preferences. This is a time to take back your preferences and to tailor your physical environment and lifestyle in ways that suit you best. Do things that make you happy. Fill your space with nourishing sights, sounds, and smells. Turn your bedroom into your sanctuary. Buy yourself a beautiful set of sheets so you feel like royalty when you crawl into bed.

Lastly, this is a good time to remind yourself to make sure you're tending to the basics. In times of upheaval or emotional distress, it's easy to neglect the necessities that support our physical and emotional wellbeing, so here is a gentle reminder of some of those basic needs:

- You need adequate sleep and a consistent sleep schedule. Deep sleep cleanses the mind and helps the psyche to assimilate unprocessed emotions and impressions. Sleep also supports a healthy lymphatic system, clear thinking, and emotional equilibrium. When possible, give yourself permission to take naps, and to sleep as much as you want and as your schedule permits.

- You need fresh, healthy food—preferably foods that are light, comforting, and easy to digest—and plenty of purified water. Cooking for yourself and indulging in the foods you love and that your body metabolizes well are intimate acts of kindness and self-love. Drinking enough water is also highly restorative and raises the vibrational frequency in both body and mind.

- Lastly, you need some form of daily movement. Getting your body moving reduces cortisol levels, enhances mood, and supports physical and emotional wellbeing. And if weather permits you to take a walk outdoors, so much the better. Fresh air is filled with negative ions that infuse your bloodstream and increase the good-mood chemical serotonin, helping to alleviate depression, alleviate stress, and boost energy.

The more you regard your home as a restorative space, the more you'll come to look forward to the simple pleasure of connecting with yourself. This is a perfect time to exercise your freedom to laugh or cry easily and without worrying about how any other person might react. It's a time to take up as much or as little space as feels right to you, and to simply exist, unimpeded by anyone else's preferences or expectations, and to learn to enjoy the comfort of your solitude.

CHAPTER 6

WITHDRAWING YOUR ENERGY

Engagement is the most fundamental form of consent. Our attention is a powerful currency, and whatever we give our attention to, we're literally nourishing with our energy and encouraging to grow. Therefore, one of the most important steps we can take whenever we recognize that a relationship is no longer healthy is to withdraw our attention.

To whatever extent you are in a position to physically remove yourself from any unhealthy person or situation, I really recommend you do so. This could take the form of canceling an upcoming trip or stating your desire to take a break in the friendship or intimate relationship. It might look like submitting a transfer request to a different department at work, calling in sick for a couple of days in a row, or requesting a temporary leave of absence. It could be as simple as making the decision to stay with a friend for a few days, to visit family out of town, or to sleep for a night or two in a hotel, a guest bedroom, or on the couch.

Giving yourself permission to withdraw from the toxic people or situations in your life is about claiming your space and asserting your right to create an environment around you that feels good and supports your wellbeing. Toward this end, I also recommend identifying some "safe havens" of privacy—both at home and at work—where you can retreat when you need to breathe deeply, gather your thoughts, acknowledge your emotions, and rebalance your energy. Your bedroom, a patio or backyard, the bathroom at work, a nearby park, or even your car can provide a much-needed respite. Taking a ten-minute drive around the block can be a lifesaver when you're feeling overwhelmed or depleted. And if in any moment it's not feasible to physically remove yourself from the unhealthy person or situation, know that you can still take meaningful steps to distance yourself mentally, emotionally, and energetically.

The Art of Withdrawal

To some extent, your attention has been displaced on the person with whom you've been engaged in an unhealthy relationship, and chances are good that you've made that person's feelings, actions, and desires more important than your own. This is a time to withdraw the energy you've been pouring into other people and to redirect it into nourishing yourself.

In any interaction, we always have a choice as to where, how, and to what degree we wish to apply our attention. And there is no better time than now to direct the lion's share of your attention upon yourself. Even something as simple as using earbuds can create a nice buffer between you and others in your environment—it gives you nearly total control of the impressions you allow into your being via your sense of hearing.

As you begin extricating yourself from the nonessential or unhealthy influences in your life, notice that you don't need to do this with a sense that you are running *from* something unwanted, but with the inner knowing that you're taking an important step toward restoring your peace of mind and your autonomy. You are running *back* to yourself, to rediscover and re-establish your own internal center of gravity.

With practice, you'll soon discover that you have the capacity to engage with another without losing touch with yourself. You can choose to remain connected—to the rise and fall of each conscious breath, to the messages that your emotions and gut feelings send you on a moment-to-moment basis, and to your own internal boundaries that uphold your sense of harmony and personal space.

Your attention is the most precious form of currency you possess. Wherever and whomever you direct your focus on, you "pay" your attention to. Withdraw your attention from any nonessential or unhealthy influence, and return your powerful gaze back onto yourself.

Seeking Solitude

Sometimes we cling to unhealthy or abusive relationships like a buoy, afraid that if we let go we'll drown in a sea of loneliness and despair. We've been conditioned into the notion that "something" is better than nothing, that any relationship is better than no relationship at all, and that being with people is somehow safer or healthier than being alone. And what's ironic is that the very solitude we resist is actually the lifeline that makes transformation possible.

Making time to be alone is a journey we take into the stillness, into the void, where we willingly release who we've been, along with our attachment to knowing who we'll be when we reemerge. I completely understand that this process may feel scary. Withdrawing our attention from the outer world in order to restore our connection with ourselves can feel like descending into a dark and mysterious tunnel. You're not sure how long the tunnel is or what you may encounter while inside. But I can promise you that this time of introspection is absolutely vital to your healing and your long-term happiness, because once you do emerge, whole and restored, and engage with others, it will be from a place of deep connection and self-knowledge. Your willingness to be alone is the lifeline to your own self-empowerment. It's one of the most necessary steps to achieving freedom from toxic relationships, because in solitude you learn to replenish your energy stores from the inside out, without relying on the energy of other people's approval or validation.

In solitude, you have the opportunity to re-examine the roles you've used thus far to define yourself—that of lover, friend, guide, or rescuer—and begin to puzzle out what it is that *you* really want out of this life. It's a time to unplug from the tendency to prioritize others, and to tune in to your own needs and desires with care and genuine curiosity. Spending time alone is the best way to become intimate with the ebb and flow of your emotions and to become skilled at interpreting the messages they are constantly giving you about how to restore your own wellbeing.

If you've ever cared for a newborn baby, you know that in the beginning, interpreting what they need can be unnerving, even terrifying. But the more time you spend with that child, the more in tune with them you become. Eventually, it gets to the point that you understand and can lovingly respond to the slightest sound or subtle grimace.

In the same way, this is a time to become intimate with the child within you; to become fluent in the language of your own needs and desires, and to give yourself the space to become familiar with the fertile landscape that is your inner world. In solitude, you have time to practice being comfortable in your own skin and to express your authentic self while being in the safety of your own company, knowing you have no one to perform for or acquiesce to.

Notice what genuinely makes you laugh and cry. What are you truly interested in? What kinds of activities and events light you up? What causes do you feel passionate about? What projects are you ready to take off the back burner? What are the things you are no longer willing to tolerate? It's finally time to redirect your focus back onto yourself, rather than making someone else's life wonderful at the expense of your own energy stores.

It really doesn't matter how you spend your alone time, as long as your intention is to connect deeply with yourself. If you're drawn to meditation, here is one that I guide my clients to use daily. You can also visit my website, at www.

RadicallyAuthenticYou.com/gift, to download a guided version or scan the QR code below.

A Healing Meditation

Begin by sitting in a comfortable position where you are free from outside distractions. Close your eyes and begin to locate your awareness within the very center of your being. Allow anything that you're feeling right now to simply be there. See if you can meet it with curiosity, acceptance, and love.

And now, shifting your awareness to your breath, take three deep, full breaths, in and out, into your belly. Feel the rise and fall in your belly, your chest, your heart.

Now imagine yourself surrounded with Divine Light that is deeply healing in nature. Envision this sphere of light calming anything that is unsettled within you. See it transmuting any outworn patterns or beliefs. Feel this Divine Light penetrating into every fiber of your being, relaxing your fight-or-flight response and turning on your parasympathetic nervous system to help you rest, digest, repair, and restore. Know that this is your time to rest, digest, repair, and restore. Just breathe deeply into that.

Ask this Divine source of light to liberate from within you any stored energy that is no longer serving you, to purify your thoughts and emotions, and to restore you in body, mind, and spirit.

For the next few minutes, simply bask in this healing energy. Bask in the deeply regenerating experience of your own attention, and notice how it feels to take this time out to tend to your inner world. Use your breath to continue calming and replenishing yourself.

And when you feel complete, take one final long moment to connect with the energy of self-appreciation and gratitude. Thank yourself for taking this opportunity to deepen your connection with yourself, to activate your intuition, and to continue building your reserves of self-love and self-trust.

Rest in this soothing state of being for as long as you wish, and when you are ready, slowly open your eyes, bringing this feeling of restoration back into this dimension of time and space.

You connecting with yourself is your main priority right now. And you simply cannot effectively go about this important work if you're always engaged in the cacophony of the outer world. There are just too many distractions pulling you in opposing directions. So give yourself permission to unplug and unwind, and make it a priority to silently commune with yourself.

You may find it helpful to imagine yourself a year from now, surrounded by people who truly feed your soul rather than by those who provide nothing more than a distraction or empty calories. Imagine yourself with your ideal partner, if that's something that you desire. See yourself being one hundred percent comfortable in your own skin, feeling fabulous about who you are and what you want, pursuing the things that matter to you, and asking for and receiving what you need.

Through your time in solitude, know that you're building a relationship with your authentic self. And once this relationship is solid, you'll no longer feel the need to put on any pretenses in any aspect of your life. You'll no longer bite your tongue or settle for less than you really desire. You are in the process of becoming someone with an unshakable sense of self-knowledge, self-respect, and self-love. A person who is at home within yourself first and foremost.

I assure you that *this* is where you're headed. And I can also tell you, there are no shortcuts. You have to actually invest the time and energy in getting to know yourself. This is one of the many gifts of being alone.

CHAPTER 7

HONORING YOUR INTUITION

Each of the pillars of restoration that we've been explor-ing in this section share a common goal. They are designed to soothe your nervous system, and in so doing, guide you back into concert with your natural state of alignment and connection, a state in which you are recep-tive enough to recognize and heed the messages from your own internal wisdom. Restoration is a process of recon-necting you with your innate guidance system, which has a highly tuned ability to discern beneficial people and experiences from those that—for you, right now—are not as beneficial.

In the same way we're born with receptors in our digestive system that interpret hunger pangs and alert us when our bodies are in need of food, we have inner indicators that lets us know whether something we're involved with or considering is for our highest good or whether it feels off. These indicators give us direct and immediate feedback—such as a sense of lightness or constriction in the body, a joyous sense of possibility in the heart or a sudden pit in the stomach. Intuition is the inner compass that helps us to ferret out when something is useful or not useful, in each unique and dynamic moment.

Intuition can be defined in a variety of different ways— as an inner knowing, a sixth sense, a "still small voice" within, or a "gut" feeling that urges us in one direction over another. Intuition is a form of direct perception that gives us knowledge of something without going through a lengthy process of analytic reasoning. Unlike the logical thought process, which can lead us down a twisting road of pros, cons, regrets, and what-ifs, intuitive signals arise more spontaneously and holistically—bypassing the logical mind and the usual machinations we use to process information. Intuition allows us to know something directly, in our bones, so to speak, without having to prove it out through the analytical process.

Intuitive knowledge is one of the purest, wisest, and most beneficial sources of intelligence that's available to us. As energetic beings living in an energetic universe, intuition is the mechanism that gives us direct access to the same stream of life-force energy that keeps our perfectly balanced solar system orbiting in perfect alignment. It's our connection to universal intelligence; our built-in guidance system that is always nudging us back in the direction of wellbeing. Each of us is born brilliantly designed to navigate life's ups and downs, and innately equipped to chart a course that will lead to our greatest expansion and joy. Intuition is our most important ally in the creation of a beautiful, fulfilling life, and this is why honing and strengthening our connection with it is so essential.

One last point about intuition, before we dive into the specifics of how to strengthen it, is that intuition is neither some woo-woo metaphysical concept, nor an elusive state that requires a psychic or a crystal ball to access. Intuition is the underpinning of our very existence, the background hum of awareness that registers even the most subtle fluctuations of comfort or tension within us. And it's always communicating with us, whether we are open to its messages or not. It's like the sun that's always shining, but we are the ones that have to open the curtains, allow it in, and benefit from its light.

Intuitive knowing is not something that has to be acquired or learned, like a foreign language or a computer program. It's something that is innate within you, always pulsating, always available, and always communicating with you. It simply needs to be understood, uncovered, celebrated, and tasked with a more primary role in our lives.

What Silences Our Inner Voice

As we explored in the first section of this book, there are many factors that we confront in our early childhood that cause us to mistrust, ignore, or even betray our "still small voice" within. These fall into a handful of categories, all of which we'll explore.

The first has to do with all the cultural and parental conditioning we receive, which lures our attention away from the rich inner world of our feelings and desires, and urges us to focus instead on being likable, being pleasing, and succeeding in the objective sense of the word.

Rushing to judgment, without giving ourselves the needed time for contemplation, is the second compelling force that seduces us away from the wisdom of our own inner guidance. The reason that we so often take off, full speed, in the wrong direction is because we're making pressured decisions and snap judgments. In other words, we don't allow ourselves adequate time to fully investigate the wisdom being transmitted to us via our emotions before committing to a certain direction. It's like we're living life as if it were some kind of timed event and we're trying to place in the top three. But there is absolutely no value in moving forward swiftly unless you've taken the time to know for certain that you have listened to yourself and that you are aligned.

A third factor in our disconnection from our wiser, intuitive knowing is something that is deeply ingrained in most women, which is our tendency to make the best of a bad situation, even if it's depleting our energy or hurting our hearts. Too often, we settle for mediocrity and take what's offered to us rather than holding out for what we really desire. In other words, we've muddled the sharp distinction between our inner *Hell Yes* and our inner *Hell No*. By the end of this section, you'll know how to clearly distinguish between the two.

A fourth obstacle to accessing intuition lies in our belief that "good" decisions are those that are based solely on the basis of logic, which causes us to pour over them incessantly. When considering a new job, or whether to begin or end a relationship, we torture ourselves with endless pros-and-cons lists, even though a much older, wiser part of us holds the answers we seek.

And lastly, we live in a culture that actually encourages us to ignore our inner world in favor of accommodating others.

Think about how many times you have heard (or thought) one of these seemingly innocuous phrases:

- After all I've done for you, how could you say no?

- You're leaving so soon?

- I went to all this trouble, and you're not even going to eat this food? (drink this drink or ... fill-in-the-blank)?

- Kiss your aunt (uncle, cousin, grandfather) goodbye.

These arbitrary rules that we live by, so woven into our daily vernacular, are not harmless. They are socially acceptable ways of disconnecting us from our own inner voice. Our conditioning pressures us to be polite even when we sense something is amiss. And if we're not vigilant, this can set us up for a lifetime of people-pleasing and self-abandoning to the point that everyone around us is well-fed with our energy and attention, but our own souls are famished and malnourished. To tip the scales back into balance, we have to take back our power from everyone and everything we've given it away to.

Reading the Room

How many times do we embark on a new relationship or situation from a state of internal turmoil? How often is our inner dialog filled with the static of self-doubt or of questioning our worthiness? And how can we expect to receive the full warmth of our intuitive, inner wisdom when our minds are chaotic and our receptors are closed down to its light? Before engaging in any new relationship or endeavor, it's so important to bring ourselves into a state of neutrality and inner calm. Only then will we be able to discern the signals and clues that are beneficial to follow, from those we'd be better off allowing to dissipate.

Reading the room is about asking ourselves the question, "How do I feel about this?" rather than, "How do others feel about me?" And then allowing ourselves to trust our instincts and first impressions rather than second-guessing them.

You see, intuition is never seduced by slick talk, fancy clothes, or someone's status or position. Only the logical mind is susceptible to those trappings.

Intuition can "see" past a person's persona and into their true nature. We just have to become open to what our intuition reveals about others, and to what others reveal about themselves. Oprah Winfrey credits Dr. Maya Angelou for teaching her one of the most important lessons of her life: "When someone tells you who they are," Dr. Angelou suggests, "believe them."

I once had a client—a very successful woman just shy of her fiftieth birthday—who quickly became infatuated with a man she believed was perfect for her. On one of their very first dates, this man, an attorney, described himself as "tenacious, relentless, and able to win in any situation." My client overturned her intuition to ask him more about these character traits, choosing instead to focus on the flower bouquets and weekend getaways he regularly showered her with, and accepted his proposal to marry him. A short two years later, my client was left not just with a broken heart, but also bankrupt. Tragically, she found out the hard way that the man she married was exactly as he had described himself: tenacious, relentless, and extremely good at winning.

How often do we find ourselves—particularly in the beginning of a relationship when hopes are high and bonding hormones are surging—confronted with a piece of information such as "I'm the jealous type," "I'm not good with commitment," or—in the case of my client—"I'm tenacious and win at all costs," but don't really take the time to inquire deeper and really allow this information to sink in? How often do we dismiss it away with comments like, "That can't be true," or "Don't say that," or, the dreaded and self-defeating, "I can change you." In actuality, this person is revealing something about themselves that our intuition picks up on as a red flag. This is where reading the room comes in. We have to be willing to listen and pause, rather than be so eager to brush our inner wisdom aside and move forward.

Intuition is the mechanism that helps us calibrate and conserve our inner and outer resources. And while there are certainly plenty of objective, logical methods for doing this—monitoring a bank account balance or planning the hours of sleep you want to get each night, for example—intuition is the only tool that can alert us to the outcome of a choice *before* we get ourselves into a financial, emotional, or energetic deficit.

By leaning into rather than pushing through a subtle feeling of tiredness, for example—the voice that says," I'd rather stay home tonight"—we are actually opening ourselves to the wisdom that lies on the other side of these sensations. Everything that arises in our bodies and minds is like a message being delivered to our door. It's wise to actually open the package and read the message before sending the messenger away.

Taking a Pause

Intuition is nourished through silence. It's revealed in stillness. Like a treasure buried deep in the ocean, its vast well of wisdom can only be accessed when the seas are calm. If the waves are turbulent, we won't be able to locate its pulsating reverberations. In order to distinguish what's a yes from what's clearly a no, we have to create a space of silence. We have to give ourselves permission to pause.

Taking a pause can be as simple as placing a hand on your heart or your belly and asking yourself, "How am I feeling right now?"

When you contemplate a particular person or course of action, does it fill you with a sense of lightness or a sense of dread? Putting all logical, practical, or worldly reasons aside, what is the energetic effect this choice is likely to have on you? Will it increase your life force, inspire you, and make you more receptive to new possibilities, or is it more likely to drain you, to muddle your clarity, or to leave you feeling bad about yourself? When you take the time to ask these questions—and more importantly, put yourself into a receiving mode so you're actually open to the answers—you will find that your broader, wiser self responds ... one hundred percent of the time.

The art of taking a pause means creating a buffer of space and time to check in with ourselves, before automatically saying yes to whatever opportunities come our way. It's resisting the temptation to make the best of something just because it's been offered.

The world's most sumptuous buffet could be set out in front of you, but if you're not hungry, then filling a plate and eating it just because it's offered will be detrimental to your wellbeing.

Even if you're presented with an opportunity for something that's universally coveted, like an all-expenses paid vacation to an exotic location, it's incredibly wise to consult your intuition before just reflexively saying yes. Maybe your soul is craving something entirely different— like a meditation retreat or a reunion with an old friend— but you won't know unless you sit with the question, unless you actually inquire.

Taking a pause is about diving into that space between the question and the answer, and asking ourselves, "In this moment, what do I really want? What am I really hungry for?" When Alan Cohen, the author of *Why Your Life Sucks: And What You Can Do About It,* wrote the words, "if it's not a hell yes, it's a hell no!" he was underlining the critical importance of giving ourselves time to actually tune in with our internal guidance system, and being willing to follow its cues. Because one thing is for certain:

If we don't give ourselves permission to pause, if we don't take the time to pull out the proverbial map to see where the train we're about to board is actually headed, we run the very real risk of repeating the same scenarios over and over again, like the movie *Groundhog Day*.

And, if something is a "maybe," or you're having trouble interpreting your feelings about a particular person or course of action, taking a pause affords you a buffer of time in order to gather more information. You are not obliged to give someone an immediate answer just because they've offered you a proposition of some kind. In fact, as we saw clearly in the first chapter of this book, emotionally unhealthy people often use love bombing in the beginning of a relationship to fast forward us past the still small voice within. And while that voice may not yet be screaming "No!" it is likely communicating something along the lines of, "Whoa, there's a lot coming at me right now and I need some time to sort it all out."

In my own life, I've put certain guidelines in place that reinforce my commitment to pausing before jumping into action. One is something I call the twenty-four-hour rule. If something is a good idea now, it will still be a good idea a day from now. When contemplating a big decision, give yourself permission to sleep on it and ask your dream state to reveal anything you may not be seeing clearly.

Noticing What You Notice

Intuition doesn't usually appear like a burning bush or a bolt of lightning. Often, it's a subtle feeling that is trying to get us to take notice—like a voice whispering, "Hey, there's something here that would be in my best interest to pay attention to." It can arise as a feeling of interest or a strong emotion in the solar plexus that lets us know there's something valuable to be mined here. *There is gold here for me.* This is why the final step to activating your intuition is to pay close attention to what lights you up. In other words, *notice what you notice.*

Pay attention to the movies you're drawn to, the music that moves you, the conversations or areas of interest that intrigue you. I call these spiritual bread crumbs. The things that interest you, captivate you, evoke curiosity or a deep emotional reaction deserve your attention, however illogical or out of the blue they may seem. By following them and noticing where they lead, you validate and strengthen your connection to your intuition.

Years ago I worked with a young woman named Brooke who mentioned during one of our sessions that she'd recently been to a wedding where all the older men performed a type of Polynesian dance to honor the bride and groom. A Jewish girl raised in West Los Angeles, Brooke had no previous connection whatsoever with Polynesian culture, but in the presence of this dance she was so deeply moved that she instantly burst into tears.

I suggested to Brooke that this spontaneous sensation of interest and affinity could be a communication from her intuition trying to lead her in the direction of some of the things she was hoping to accomplish through our coaching work together—namely, to meet more like-minded people, to find activities that would leave her feeling joyful and carefree outside of the club scene, and to improve her physical fitness.

I urged Brooke to indulge her interest in this new culture; to read up on it, to watch videos, and to explore where in her community something similar might be offered. I reassured her that it wasn't necessary to have a logical reason for pursuing this interest, and that it didn't matter if it paid off right away—or ever. What was important was to recognize this as an invitation—delivered to her directly from life—to begin listening for and following her deeper passions, and allowing her inner wisdom to chart the course to the next phase in her life.

I received an email from Brooke a few months later, updating me on the ways her life had changed and thanking me for supporting her in following this hunch with an open mind. In the email she shared that she began taking lessons in Polynesian dance, which had led her not only to meeting a whole new and interesting group of people her age but also contributed to her fitness and the healthy lifestyle she'd been craving. In retrospect, she could see that her interest in this subject was in fact a spiritual bread crumb, and she was grateful that she made the choice to see where it led her rather than allowing her logical mind to talk her out of it.

One of the beautiful things about intuition is that it is perfectly, sublimely, intelligently self-serving. Meaning that its sole purpose is to support, enhance, and protect the care and thriving of YOU. It is on your side, always, seeking endlessly creative ways to support you in caring for the sacred temple that is your heart, mind, and body.

No other soul has incarnated into the exact energetic frequency that is you. No one else knows the intricacies of your life experiences, nor your reaction to those experiences. No one but you has the ability to calibrate the distance between where you are and where you want to be. No one else but you can interpret the billions of responses that are firing off, moment by moment, in your body and mind, and no one but you is more perfectly qualified to bring your body-mind system back into balance when something has knocked you off. You are the only person who can make the choice to swim out in the direction of your interests and honor your callings.

Intuition is the vehicle that allows us to distinguish the parts of ourselves and our lives that are longing to be nurtured into being from the aspects that are in the process of dying. And really, what more essential skill could any of us possibly develop than the sensitivity to know when to end a relationship that's about to lead us into despair, to quit the job that's sucking our souls, and even to ditch the eating plan or exercise regime that's no longer supporting who we are now? These are our inborn navigational skills, and if nourished and sharpened, they will lead us to the most life-giving options, naturally and effortlessly.

It is my firm personal and deeply held spiritual belief that the Divine energy of light and wellbeing abounds in this Universe. Literally, this is the stuff life is made of and this energy exists in limitless supply. Life force energy runs in wide, abundant currents and streams, always available to bathe us in its vitality, creativity, and healing inspiration. But we are the ones who must make our way to the river's edge. Intuition is this guide.

The last thing I'll say for now about intuition is that it's not something you can consult with just once. It's not a "set it and forget it" type of deal. It's an ongoing relationship that you must attend to daily and even minute by minute. And please don't gaslight yourself if you thought you were listening to your intuition, but the situation played out in such a way that you later realized you weren't really connected. Intuition works in hindsight too, and the view gained from the rearview mirror of our lives is as valuable as the view from the front windshield.

If you were to look back on some of the most meaningful experiences of your life—both positive and negative—you will recognize the presence of your inner guidance. In particular, you will recognize it in the experiences you've had with emotionally abusive individuals. You may even recall specific ways that your inner guidance attempted to communicate with you. Through steps and missteps alike we come to intimately recognize that voice within us.

Think about it this way: A good friendship is forged because of good and bad times alike, and the same is true with the friendship you are developing with your intuition. So if you're off—if you zig where you would have been better to zag—recognize and give yourself credit for the aha that you had about it in hindsight.

The fact is, this deeper, wiser, broader part of you has been with you all along. It was there during the chaos of your childhood and in the lost years of young adulthood. It was with you in every traumatic, toxic, and/or abusive relationship you've ever lived through, and it was also there, high-fiving you, during every high-minded experience and great decision you've ever created for yourself.

It's time to reprogram yourself to listen to the voice of your powerful inner guidance. And just like building a muscle, your ability to hear it will get more robust and more precise over time. Just make a commitment to taking time to listen and to taking whatever action steps it urges you toward. Soon its momentum will carry you and you will trust that your inner wisdom is accessible anytime and anywhere you go.

CHAPTER 8

ESTABLISHING RIGOROUS BOUNDARIES

Ultimately, this book is a conversation about self-love, not as a vague concept or some lofty ideal, but as a daily and even moment-to-moment awareness and commitment. And our personal boundaries are one of the most direct reflections of our degree of self-love. Nothing else intimately correlates our self-esteem, our sense of self-worth, and our access to our personal empowerment than our ability to identify and maintain our own personal boundaries.

By its very definition, a boundary is something that indicates a border or limit. It's a line of demarcation that distinguishes us from others and from the world around us. Our boundaries are the physical, emotional, and mental limits we establish to communicate who we are, what we think, how we feel, and what we will and will not tolerate, independent of the thoughts, feelings, preferences, and behaviors of others. Our boundaries form the metaphoric and sometimes literal line in the sand where those around us end, and we begin.

For many of us, considering ourselves as separate individuals—with needs, preferences, ideas, and desires that are distinct from those around us—is not something we're in the habit of doing. Thanks in part to messages such as "Children should be seen and not heard," "Big boys don't cry," and "Mind your manners," that were ingrained in so many of us early on, we literally never learned the importance of distinguishing who we are, what we're interested in, and what we prefer. Our preferences need to be independent of the opinions of those around us. In fact, many of us have formed our very identities around our ability to empathize, to accommodate, to go with the flow, and to be flexible and adaptive to the needs of others. And if this description is central to your self-definition, I want to urge you to use this time to dive deeper.

You are a unique individual with ideas of your own; these deserve to be explored and expressed. You have interests, preferences, and passions that have arisen as a result of a lifetime of experiences, and these deserve to be given attention and priority. You also have aversions and deal breakers, also borne from your direct personal experience, that are not there by accident, but are a valuable part of your awakening wisdom. Your boundaries are a lifeline, and when you don't take the time to clarify them—or when you deny or downplay them for the sake of pleasing others—you deprive the world of getting to know your true, authentic self. And it is your authentic self that you seek, for this foundation is essential to your freedom, your satisfaction, and your self-expression.

Distinguishing Your "Hell Yes" from Your "Hell No"

Our personal boundaries create a line of protection and support around the unique individuals that we are. And as such, our boundaries help to shield us from being manipulated, used, or violated by others—whether by accident or on purpose. Good boundaries allow us to feel safe, protected, and nourished. Boundaries communicate to our inner self that we are important. That we are valuable. And that we are worthy of our own care and consideration. In fact, every time we set and maintain a healthy boundary, we are reinforcing our self-worth. And every time we deny our truth—every time we say yes when we mean no or no when we mean yes—we weaken our self-worth.

And so the question naturally arises: If boundaries are so essential to our physical, mental, emotional, financial, and spiritual wellbeing, why do so many of us have such difficulty establishing and maintaining them?

As we've already explored, those of us who grew up in chaotic or unstable environments often learned to survive by prioritizing other people's needs and emotions, usually by disconnecting from our own. We learned to give up our personal space—both literally and figuratively—in the service of other people's happiness. And because this is what feels "normal" to us, it's easy to carry these patterns into our adult relationships.

In other words, those of us with unhealthy, loose, or poorly defined boundaries often violate our own space and blow past our values and limitations in the name of pleasing others or keeping the peace. In a sense, we betray ourselves in an attempt to prove our loyalty, and therefore our value, to another. And while it may seem in the moment that it's simply easier to bend to the will of others than to stand our ground, the relinquishment of our personal boundaries is incredibly detrimental to living the authentic lives we long for.

We have to bear in mind that because emotional abuse is more subtle and insidious than physical abuse, it often involves our boundaries being violated in imperceptible increments. Sometimes our nervous system becomes so overwhelmed that we can't quite put our fingers on what is happening in the moment. We are like that proverbial frog in the pot slowly boiling on the stove. In the beginning, we may not be able to pinpoint exactly what's happening, but we're very clear that it doesn't feel good: it seems off in some fundamental way. Often it's only in hindsight that we're able to appreciate the fact that an important boundary has been crossed, or, more accurately, that we've allowed an important boundary to be crossed.

What you stand to gain from this essential exploration of your personal boundaries is the knowledge, understanding, and wisdom to become an expert on yourself. And this knowledge is fundamental: You *want* to truly understand what makes you tick, what causes you to contract and shut down, and what lights you up and makes your heart sing. Armed with this foundation of self-knowledge, self-acceptance, and self-respect, we naturally attract those into our lives who feel likewise about themselves and others. And when we don't operate from this foundation of self-knowledge and self-love, we simply can't resonate with people who do. If we break our promises to ourselves, we set the stage for others to break their promises to us. As the old adage goes, if you have a low opinion of yourself, you'll find others who will agree. The act of identifying and setting boundaries forces us to get real with ourselves. The process provides us with an incredibly valuable opportunity to clarify what we prefer, what and whom we wish to participate with, and what we absolutely will not tolerate.

There is no better time than the present to begin clarifying your important boundaries. Unless you get clear about who you now are, what you now want, and what it is you are right now seeking to bring into your life, you could spend years saying yes to a whole lot of people and activities when you should actually say, "Hell no!"

It can be so easy to say yes to situations and relationships simply because they provide a distraction, or because, in the short term at least, being with someone feels better than being alone. It's easy to say yes to avoid actually having to look within, and keep ourselves busy in order to minimize or deny the aspects of ourselves that legitimately need our energy, nurturance, and healing. But when we agree to things simply because they're convenient, or as ways of running from our deeper selves, we end up creating the same unfulfilling experiences over and over, whether with the same people or with a new cast of characters.

Now is the time to reverse this trend, and to begin creating your life on purpose, from the inside out, and in a way that honors the unique individual that you are. And this begins with an honest acknowledgment of what I call your "key areas of discontent."

Identifying Key Areas of Discontent

While there are many ways to begin the process of clarifying personal boundaries, one of the most immediately beneficial is to start with the areas where you're already experiencing some level of discontent. Because regardless of what aspects of life you're struggling with, these areas always reveal places where clearer personal boundaries are needed.

Think of any aspects of your life where you find yourself complaining, and particularly where you've had chronic or long-standing complaints. In which relationships do you feel trapped, powerless, obligated, or without choice? Where are you holding resentment? In what aspects of your life are you frequently dissatisfied or feel low-key pissed off about much of the time? In what relationships do you feel unseen, unappreciated, or disrespected? Where and with whom have you been repeatedly disappointed, deceived, or heartbroken? In what relationships or situations do you feel continually uncomfortable or irritated? The answers to these questions are all very rich places for self-discovery, because, regardless of what the other people involved are doing or not doing, the areas where you consistently struggle always reflect undefined or unenforced boundaries.

And here I want to say that the process of discovering where your own boundaries need shoring up is *not* about excusing or condoning the bad behavior of others. And it's also not about blaming or condemning those others. Both of these perspectives keep us powerless and at the mercy of others. Clarifying our boundaries is first and foremost about taking responsibility for ourselves and our lives as they exist in this moment, and then using the information gained to do a better job of caring for ourselves so we can create what we desire from this point forward.

And so I invite you to simply notice, to see, and to become informed by the areas in your life where you're currently aware that you're not getting all that you desire, where you don't feel things are equitable, and most importantly, where you feel like your light is being dimmed. And then, like any good parent would, become willing to set boundaries in these areas because you are unwilling to tolerate *any* further diminishment of your light.

Acknowledging What Makes You Unique

We are each born with certain unique gifts. We've each endured unique losses. We each have highly individualized hopes and desires, and we've each lived through some degree of trauma. These are vital parts of what makes us who we are, and all of it deserves to be honored and respected.

Some of us struggle with addiction or have been close to someone who has. And those who do will naturally need more robust boundaries around the using of potentially addictive substances. Some of us were born with a higher-than-average sensitivity to other people's energy or to noise or to other environmental influences. Some of us need more solitude, more personal space, or more time to think things through than those around us. Some of us can't go a day without listening to music, being in nature, writing, singing, painting, or indulging some other creative expression. Some of us may need to follow a diet that deviates significantly from the typical American mainstay in order for our bodies to thrive.

Whatever your unique peculiarities, the discovery of them is amazing news! It means that your ability to care for yourself, skillfully and intelligently, has just increased exponentially.

Your strengths and weaknesses alike are part of what makes you uniquely you. Now is the time to acknowledge these so you can begin attending to your own needs without any justification or apology. Once you understand and find acceptance for that which makes you unique, you can fly your flag proudly! You can begin sorting for those who are naturally aligned with your needs and preferences, and allowing those who don't to simply pass through your experience. And one thing is assured: Those who resonate with who you are and what you're up to will gravitate toward you, and those who don't will move out of your experience. This is the way the universe sorts things out for our highest benefit. But in order for the universe to work on our behalf, we must be honest about who we are and what we need. Identifying your unique lifestyle preferences is another important way to begin clarifying and refining your boundaries.

Honoring Your Physical, Emotional, and Spiritual Values

Physically, we are each entitled to a certain amount of personal space, and we're entitled to physical safety, comfort, and wellbeing. This includes and is not limited to the food we eat; the ways and frequency with which we move our physical bodies; the amount of sleep, reflection or downtime we require; and the ability to choose what types of media and other images we consume.

Our emotional or energetic boundaries should reflect what feels good to us and the influences we desire to include within our psychic or energetic space. To clarify them, spend some time exploring what feels good to you energetically and emotionally, as well as noticing what you may be allowing into your life that doesn't feel good.

Journaling and freewriting are excellent ways to discover the things that feed your soul. Begin with prompts such as, "I love ..." "I'm passionate about ..." "Something that inspires me is ..." or "I feel great about myself when I ..." Create a list of activities and environments that easily nourish your self-esteem and vitality, and make sure your lifestyle is set up to include a healthy diet of them.

Likewise, spend some time contemplating what environments, activities, and people consistently leave you feeling sad, anxious, or drained of energy, and give yourself permission to limit your contact—at least temporarily—with these unhealthy influences.

The following is a good journaling prompt to help you set robust boundaries around the influences that may be robbing you of energy: "To preserve my energy, it's okay for me to ..." Then read this list often to further acknowledge and affirm your innate right to do what feels best to you. Robust boundaries aren't just essential for protecting our physical and emotional wellbeing; they also remind us to nourish our spirits.

The concept of spiritual boundaries is not frequently talked about, but basically these include rituals, practices, and lifestyle choices that honor your connection with the non-physical essence of you, whether you refer to this as your soul or spirit, Source energy, God, life force, infinite intelligence, or whether you have no name whatsoever to describe this unbounded part of yourself. Spiritual boundaries uphold your right to believe whatever you believe, and to organize your life to align with those beliefs. For example, your spiritual boundaries may inform the types of food you eat or the environments you prefer to eat them in. They may influence how (or if) you participate with certain holidays, and they will certainly influence those whose counsel you seek.

You can always turn to your intuition and gut instincts to help you discern the true nature of people and organizations alike; just because something or someone calls themselves "spiritual" doesn't make it so. Something is spiritual if it uplifts your vibration and causes your spirit to soar.

Identifying Your Deal Breakers

The above exploration will guide you to identify your long-standing complaints, your deeply held values, and the particular assets and oddities that make you uniquely you. Armed with this information, a clear picture of your "hell nos." or deal breakers will naturally emerge.

Your deal breakers refer to aspects of yourself and your lifestyle that are nonnegotiable. These are the things that must be present, or must *not* be present, for you to be at your best—physically, emotionally, mentally, and spiritually. For example, for some people, daily physical exercise is a deal breaker; it's something they're simply not willing to live without. And if they fail to honor this boundary, their self-esteem and mood plummet, their vitality suffers, and their resilience in handling all types of situations and challenges is greatly diminished. We each have these types of deal breakers, and the more up front we are about them, the more grief we'll save ourselves in the long run.

To become conscious about the deal breakers you may not have previously acknowledged, you can begin by asking yourself questions such as, *What people, activities, and previous commitments are no longer enjoyable or life-giving? What hobbies, habits, or pastimes have I outgrown or am no longer interested in? What activities and relationships leave me feeling worse about myself and my life than I did before I engaged with them? What am I ready to let go of?*, and, *What am I no longer willing to tolerate?* These are the specific lines in the sand that are yours to clarify, and to communicate to others in your life.

Communicating Your Boundaries

By far the most significant part of creating personal boundaries is the inner work each of us must do to clarify what's truly important to us. Oftentimes this inner clarity is enough, as our energy and presence speak volumes about who we are and what we value. But when misunderstandings, disappointments, or hurt feelings arise regularly, it's usually an indication that we need to do a better job in communicating our boundaries.

Perhaps the most helpful tip I can offer is to take some time, before you set out to communicate your boundaries, to get firmly grounded within yourself as to *why* this limit is important to you. Your why is the most important component of any boundary you're seeking to implement. Getting clear about what you stand to gain from putting this boundary in place, and what you stand to lose if you don't, supplies the inspiration you need to effectively communicate your values with the important people in your life.

Every boundary you create is in service to this deeper why. For example, if you have a boundary about going to bed at a particular time, this boundary is most likely not arbitrary. In fact, it's probably a direct result of some specific wisdom you've gained as a result of your personal life experience. And it probably also reflects a goal you are working toward. The why in this case is what you are hoping to achieve through the observance of this boundary. "I like waking up refreshed rather than sluggish" might be the reason underlying this particular boundary. The more connected you are to this underlying why, the more you increase your chances of honoring the boundaries you've created for yourself, and the more articulate you'll be when communicating them to others.

Communicating your boundaries will go better if you use "I" statements rather than "you" statements. For example, "I need some time alone to unwind after work," as opposed to "You need to stop talking to me the minute I get home." Remember, in sharing your boundaries, you're giving those in your life high-quality information about who you are, what you need, what doesn't work for you, and what makes you outrageously happy. Both the giving and the receiving of this information is an act of generosity, so do your best to communicate it with diplomacy and grace.

One final point about communicating your boundaries is that it's not necessary to present the entirety of your reasoning or the detailed backstory about how this boundary came to be important to you. In fact, the more time you spend justifying your boundary the less effective your communication becomes. Remember that your boundary is simply a limit that you're establishing to support yourself in living in alignment with the person you desire to be. This vision of your best self is what's important to communicate, not all the trials and tribulations you may have gone through to clarify it.

The restorative practices offered in this section of the book are all designed to support you in creating a more harmonic energetic baseline within yourself. As a result of trying them on and integrating them into your life, you're discovering what it feels like to stand in your truth, to be authentically yourself, to operate with a calm—not frenetic—nervous system, and to attend to your moment-to-moment connection with yourself as your highest priority. And from this place of neutrality and sovereignty, you are now ready to rebuild your life on a more solid foundation. This foundation supports all that you are and all that you desire, and honors all that you know now as a result of all that you have lived. So let the building begin!

PART III

RECLAIM

CHAPTER 9

RETRIEVING THE TREASURES

If Part Two was the process of deconstructing—of clearing away the psychic rubble and standing again on fertile soil—then Part Three is a process of rebuilding on that newly leveled ground. And this rebuilding is very different from the act of constructing a persona for the purpose of getting others to love, accept, or validate us. It's a conscious creation that we undertake from the sobriety of knowing who we truly are, what we need, and what will actually work for us at this significant turning point in our lives.

It's time now to construct a personal operating system that is based on the unique wisdom you have gained through your own life experience and self-examination. And for better or for worse, no teacher or book can adequately convey this wisdom. Only life can teach it to us. We gather it from kissing our share of frogs, from recognizing ourselves as that frog in the bubbling pot, and from summoning the resolve to extricate ourselves yet again from unhealthy dynamics and situations. And what we come to discover is that every one of these situations and relationships has served us.

Each and every relationship you've attracted to your-self—and each and every time you opted for a choice that took you further away from your internal sense of home—you gathered valuable wisdom and self-awareness. It's now time to unpack that wisdom and put it to use, to rewrite your story from that of victim to victor, and reclaim your power to create your life. Because every heartbreak, every path taken and not taken, has been leading you to the full sovereignty of yourself: to the reclamation of your light.

You see, we don't just choose unhealthy partners to soothe us from feelings of loneliness or unworthiness. We choose them because we're afraid of owning our full potential, claiming all of our personal power, and standing in all of our light. We linger too long in relationships with those who are not up to par with us—spiritually, intellectually, socially, or financially—because we were not ready to embody all of who we are. We're not yet ready to proclaim our greatness and stand in all our power, so we couple with people who cast a shadow over our lives. And in in this way, we actually *are* a perfect vibrational match with the emotional abuser, for they also seek to diminish our light.

What I hope you are now beginning to realize is that each of us is responsible for creating the space for our authentic self to emerge. We are each responsible for bring-ing forth our light, and for discerning the people, causes, and intentions we want to give our energy to, as well as those we wisely choose to withdraw our energy from.

And so, this is a time for reclamation. This is the time to celebrate what has truly been a hero's journey: to acknowledge your triumphant passage from victimhood to survivorship and beyond. From pain to greater purpose.

In reclaiming the fullness of your wisdom and light, you will naturally mourn all the times you allowed others to diminish it. You may rage at all the times you weren't heard, and your needs and preferences were not honored. Your heart may break as you acknowledge all the times you settled for far less than what you truly desire and deserve. You may recoil as you think of all the energy you expended trying your very best to make a satisfying meal out of absolute scraps, of all the times you engaged in conversations you knew would go nowhere, and of all the times you pretended to be interested in things that bored the ass right off you.

These choices were rooted in fear and scarcity: *If I let this guy go, will there ever be anyone else? If I fire this employee, I'll never find someone to replace them.* Ultimately, we stay in unhealthy relationships and situations long after their expiration date because we believe they were all we deserve, or all the universe has in store for us.

As part of the reclamation process, you may mourn the aspects of yourself that you pretended did not exist: the sophisticated, sensitive, quirky, genius parts of yourself you tried to hide from view lest they upset the apple-cart of the dysfunctional relationship you were trying to keep intact. You may mourn the brilliant human being that, until now, was not given permission to shine. And then, you will simply go about the business of reclaiming your light.

What you'll discover is that the pain of losing yourself is never for naught, because the joy of finding yourself makes the entire journey worthwhile. You can never know the relief of returning home, unless you've known the gnawing discomfort of having strayed. You can never know and appreciate the fullness of who you are unless you've settled for far less. The comfort of returning to your authentic self is even more exquisite once you've known the discomfort of concealing it behind a facade.

I'm reminded of my dear friend Justin who walked into my house one day with a yoga mat slung around his shoulder, donning a pair of metallic blue bike shorts about three sizes too small for him. He had been so captivated by a gorgeous woman he'd met who owned a yoga studio that he immediately began conforming his personality to fit the mold of a yogi, the type of man he was convinced he would need to become to spark her interest.

The moment Justin and I locked eyes, we erupted into a long, deep, side-splitting laugh. Justin is a brilliant businessman and an avid rock climber, hiker, and outdoorsman, but he's no yogi. He was powerfully attracted to this woman's physical beauty and poise, and because of the physical attraction, he naturally assumed that the two were spiritually, intellectually, socially, and financially aligned as well. They were not. And Justin tucked away many of his most authentic and delicious character traits during the three months he dated her.

The special irony of this experience is that the word "yoga" is related to the word "yoke," which means equally aligned, and similar in values, lifestyle, and beliefs. How many times do we assume that just because we feel resonance with someone on one level—such as physical attraction—that we are aligned in deeper and more meaningful ways? And how many times do we take on the value system of a friend, co-worker, or a lover, simply because we haven't yet taken the time to get clear about what our own values are?

So it's time to rediscover who you are, distinct from everything you have been or pretended to be in the past. It's time to reclaim the parts of yourself you put on the back burner, zipped into too-tight jeans, or otherwise kept a lid on. Breathe deeply, because it's time now to joyously unwind yourself from whatever pretzel shape you may have twisted yourself into to fit within your previous relationships. You're about to feel how freeing it is to reclaim the truth of who you are, be okay with it, and fly your flag high and proud. By taking the time to discover your personal value system and then evaluate those who enter your life in relation to those values, you can immediately see where there is alignment and where you are about to sell out who you are and what's important to you.

Every time you go through a difficult or trying experience, you earn what I think of as "spiritual bonus points." They are like gifts given by the universe, from the Divine. Every experience leaves you with valuable awareness, insights, skills, and wisdom you simply wouldn't have developed had you not been put to that particular test. It's a little like earning points in a video game: the resources and skills you acquire at one skill level equip you to master the next level of the game. Greater clarity about your core values and greater access to Divine guidance are two of these precious gifts.

CHAPTER 10

FINDING YOUR TRUE NORTH

Imagine if you'd been born with an internal homing device or GPS that was constantly beaming a signal to guide you from wherever you are to wherever you wanted to be? What if you had access to an inner compass that could always point you in the direction of your own personal True North? A compass that would lead you in the direction of your alignment, your happiness, and your inner peace? Well, the great news is you *were* born with such a compass. It's made up of your most deeply held values, aspirations, and the principles you desire to live by and to make manifest in the world and in your life.

Uncovering, clarifying, and declaring your unique and personal values will serve you in so many ways. First, in a very real sense, your values act as your personal orienting point in a world that's constantly spinning with all manner of diverse intentions and desires. Next, your values act as a kind of homing device that can not only chart your course toward where you want to go but can also illumine the way back if you become confused or feel you've gone astray.

Then, once you're clear about the qualities you deeply value and want to encourage to flourish in your life, this clarity acts like a filtration system, helping you to sift through an endless number of people, ideas, situations, and opportunities, and to align only with those that will uplift, evolve, and inspire you, rather than those that may look good on the surface, but will actually deplete you.

And lastly, your values—or, more accurately, the level to which you choose to value yourself—determines how much or how little of life's banquet you're able to attract to yourself and allow yourself to receive. To value yourself highly is to establish your personal vibration in a bandwidth of frequency where love, abundance, freedom, safety, and authenticity flow into and out of your experience naturally and easily. Self-knowledge, combined with self-worth and self-love, allows us to see clearly those paths that will support our fulfillment and continued growth, and to steer clear of those that will bring us down or diminish our light.

Flying Blind

Most of us are still being guided by values that aren't necessarily of our own conscious choosing: they've been handed down to us by others and we picked them up by default. Rather than being guided by our inner True North, we have allowed ourselves to be influenced by other people's ideas and intentions, which may or may not be aligned with our own.

Our values get instilled within us by well-meaning and not so well-meaning others: caregivers, peers, lovers, government, religious institutions, employers, Hollywood, and mass media, just to name a few. And because the messages we receive from these sources are often conflicting, they can leave us feeling unsure about how to proceed and at risk of aligning with a certain train of thought and/or course of action simply because that's the voice that is urging us the loudest.

Without clarity about what we truly value, we are prone to navigating our lives according to whatever path seems the easiest, or promises us security, validation, acceptance, or any of the other things that the wounded part of us craves. And unless we take the time to uninstall these values and instill new ones in their place, they will continue to run in the background of our human operating system, like an outdated app on your cell phone that pulls focus away from more important tasks and drains battery life.

Once you uncover them, your unique values will become your dearest friend and trusted compass, always available to help you navigate toward your own True North, and always leading you toward living a reclaimed, authentic life.

The Correlation Between Values, Vibration, and Receiving

We live in a universe of energy and vibration, in which all things come together and manifest through a process of attraction. Everything in this seemingly material universe is made of energy, and like energies are attracted to one another because they are similar in frequency and resonance.

Our thoughts vibrate at certain frequencies. Our emotions vibrate at certain frequencies. And the way we think and feel about ourselves generates a wave of energy that is felt by all we encounter and determines in large part the types of experiences we draw into our lives. You see, in this vibrational universe, we don't automatically match up with everyone and everything. We match up with what we focus our energy and attention upon. We match what we vibrate in harmony with.

Our values directly impact our vibration, because our values correlate with what we think we do and don't deserve. Our values reveal what we believe is available to us and what we've decided is out of our reach. It's like life is this lavish, fully stocked buffet, but most of the time our value system limits us to ordering off a tiny menu that consists only of what we are able to see at any moment. But as this beautiful poem, written in the early 1900s by poet Jessie Rittenhouse, suggests, we are the ones who set the level of the bar in accordance with what we value and what we believe about our financial prosperity, our career success, and most certainly about our relationships with others.

I bargained with Life for a penny,
And Life would pay no more,
However I begged at evening
When I counted my scanty store;

For Life is just an employer,
He gives you what you ask,

But once you have set the wages,
Why, you must bear the task.

I worked for a menial's hire,
Only to learn, dismayed,
That any wage I had asked of Life,
Life would have paid.

This poem, which I first came across years ago in Napoleon Hill's classic *Think and Grow Rich*, is now dog-eared, underlined, and highlighted, because it reinforces something I have always known to be true: Life always says yes.

The universe will yield to us that which we are clearly and vibrationally aligned to. This well-stocked kitchen—meaning this universe and all the experiences that are possible to create within it—is limitless. Its cupboards and shelves are filled with every conceivable experience, relationship, opportunity, and possibility we can imagine, and in every conceivable combination. But here's the rub. We attract from this great bountiful universe only what we are honed onto vibrationally. We attract only the level of quality in all things that we believe we are deserving of receiving.

This is why lazy focus and undefined preferences get us into so much trouble. In the analogy of the well-stocked kitchen, if we're a "yes" to everything in the cupboard, then we have no way of ensuring that what gets delivered to our table will actually be satisfying, healthy, or even safe for us to consume. If we haven't yet clarified what we want enough to differentiate it from what we don't want, we give away our power and creative control over what and who we draw into our lives.

It's Time to Raise Your Standards, Girl!

In 2003, after going through my first divorce, I felt extremely disconnected from my True North and was very much in need of direction and guidance. Not yet having access to the inner tools that I now keep front and center in my tool chest, I visited every astrologer, tarot reader, and psychic who landed on my radar, hoping for some clarity. Actually, if I'm being perfectly honest, I wanted someone to tell me the details about my next relationship: *When would I meet this person, how would I meet him, and what will he be like?* Husband number one didn't work out, so clearly it was time to dust myself off, get back on the horse, and track down my soul mate, right?

That's when I met Randy.

Randy was larger than life—funny, charismatic, and straight to the point. I liked him instantly. He was also a very gifted intuitive. When I sat down for a psychic reading with Randy, he took one look at me and said, "Honey, you say yes to anything the universe sends you! Whatever falls off the shelf as you're rolling by, you put in your shopping cart and start dating it! How can the universe send you someone really wonderful when you say yes to everyone? It's time to raise your standards, girl." This was by far the best advice I'd ever received up to that point, and it became the launching point of me defining who I was and what I valued—not from the perspective of a wounded girl, but from that of a wiser and more seasoned woman.

Because here's the thing. Unless we deliberately decide what we want, what we don't want, what we are willing to work toward, and what we absolutely will not tolerate, we will attract people and experiences based on an old, outdated, and most likely undesirable vibration. Without clarity about what we value, we are adrift in a raging sea, constantly getting swept up in the currents around us.

Defining our values is how we carve out our own unique life path as distinct from the paths of those around us. Our values comprise a map that guides us to create our lives in harmony with what we desire. And so, if we are not yet experiencing all that we desire or deserve, we can be sure of one thing: It's time to broaden our perspective, clarify our values, raise our standards, and ask more from life. This is what you stand to gain from clarifying your values.

Prior to my fateful encounter with Randy, I thought clarifying values was an intellectual experience—like declaring that you want to date a professional who checks all the boxes and looks good on paper. But the values clarification process is more than simply making a laundry list of what you're looking for in a house or a job or a companion. It goes so much deeper than that.

Clarifying your values is like choosing the particular tone you wish to harmonize with and play as the background music of your life. It's sounding a clarion call into the universe that announces your intention to usher in a new way of living. It's identifying the principles you want to live by, and integrating those principles so well into the fabric of your thinking, your outlook, your daily actions, and your very being that it changes the vibrational signal you are sending out. So that's what we're up to at this point in the process.

The Values Clarifying Process Step-by-Step: Uncovering Your Nonnegotiable Six Values

I recommend you start this process by reflecting on the following list of approximately a hundred core values, in order to gain an overview of the particular frequency you're seeking to nurture in your life at this time. The intention of this first part of the process is to get your creative juices flowing and to possibly expand the range of values that you already know are important to you.

I understand that the size of this list may be daunting at first, but it will feel less so if you think of it simply as variety. The fact is each of us is born with incredibly unique interests and inclinations, and the life experiences we gather along our journey make us even more so. And as a result, the spectrum of values that we come to hold dear is virtually endless. So, think of this list like a menu to the enormous smorgasbord of values and qualities that you could choose to build your life around. Use it as a starting point, circling, starring, or writing on a separate piece of paper the twenty or so qualities out of the hundred that you most wish to embody in your life *at this time.*

And please note that the phrase "at this time" is important, because all I'm asking you to consider in this process is this particular period in your life. You don't need to take into consideration the values you had as a child, or carry forward the qualities that were important to you when your own children were young. You don't even need to consider the values you lived by last year, or those you feel will be important to you ten years from now. Just think in terms of this new moment and what you want to create from this point forward.

Also, before you begin this process, please know that there are no right or wrong answers. There is no one-size-fits-all value system that will support all people, and this process is not about creating any type of moral hierarchy. You are seeking only to identify those qualities that nurture you, inspire you, and support you in being one hundred percent authentically who you are. With this in mind, go ahead and write down your Top Twenty Values, using the list that follows as a guide (and please note, this is by no means a comprehensive list, so feel free to add any words or phrases that hold meaning for you):

Abundance, Advancement, Adventure, Affection, Altruism, Appreciation, Authenticity, Balance, Beauty, Career, Caring, Charisma, Clarity, Commonality, Communication, Community, Compassion, Connection, Contentment, Contribution, Cooperation, Courage, Creativity, Depth, Diversity, Ease, Effectiveness, Encouragement, Entertainment, Entrepreneurship, Evolution, Excellence, Excitement, Expression, Faith, Fame, Family, Fitness, Flexibility, Forgiveness, Freedom,

Friendship, Fun, Gender Expression, Generosity,
Gratitude, Happiness, Harmony, Healthy
Lifestyle, Home, Honesty, Humanity, Humor,
Independence, Innovation, Integrity, Intelligence,
Intimacy, Intuition, Invention, Involvement,
Joy, Justice, Kindness, Knowledge, Leadership,
Learning, Lightheartedness, Love, Loyalty,
Openness, Order, Partnership, Patience, Peace,
Personal Development, Playfulness, Power,
Prosperity, Providing, Purity, Relationships,
Renewal, Professionalism, Quality, Reciprocity,
Religion, Respect, Safety, Security, Self-Respect,
Sexuality, Service, Silence, Simplicity, Sobriety,
Spirituality, Strength, Success, Surrender,
Teamwork, Trust, Trustworthiness, Wealth,
Wellness, Wisdom.

During the snapshot in time when I was writing this book, I took myself through this process, and identified the following values as my current Top Twenty Values (and please note that they are listed in alphabetical order, not necessarily in their order of importance to me):

Authenticity

Balance

Communication

Family

Fitness

Freedom

Friendship

Healthy Lifestyle

Home

Humor

Honesty

Joy

Loyalty

Patience

Personal Development

Prosperity

Respect

Self-respect

Spirituality

Trust

Your Top Twenty Values serve as a general guidepost. They get you into the ballpark, so to speak, of identifying the kind of person you wish to embody and express in your life at this time. As you read through your list of twenty, you're affirming who you are and what's important to you. The next step in the process is to move from this general idea to a more specific vision of the life you desire to create.

Here is the clarity that emerged when I edited my list of Top Twenty Values down to my Top Ten Values. Their numeric order indicates their importance to me:

1. *Authenticity*

2. *Family*

3. *Healthy Lifestyle*

4. *Freedom*

5. *Spirituality*

6. *Personal Development*

7. *Trust*

8. *Respect*

9. *Communication*

10. *Honesty*

Notice that my list of ten is a more refined version of my list of twenty. It's a more essential representation of what I truly desire to live by.

To refine your list from your Top Twenty Values to your Top Ten Values, think in terms of the state-of-being you wish to embody, rather than a particular set of circumstances you'd like to create. For example, "humor" is one of my Top Twenty Values that didn't make the cut when I refined the list down to ten. And this is because humor is a condition that naturally arises when I'm being authentically who I am and expressing myself freely. While it's something I absolutely love and enjoy, it's not something I need to focus on in its own right. Rather, the vibrations of authenticity and freedom will naturally lend themselves to frequent bouts of laughter. This is an example of drilling down into your values, past the circumstances that you believe will sustain them, to the core vibration you are truly reaching for.

Let's look at another example, which is a continuation of the story I told you in the previous chapter about my friend Justin, who concluded that he should take up yoga to impress the beautiful young yoga teacher he had just met.

"Healthy Lifestyle" is one of Justin's core values, and he manifests this value in a number of ways: He exercises and meditates daily, meets with an executive coach weekly to expand his perspective and manage stress, and is extremely committed to eating only fresh, locally grown organic food. Given that "Health" is one of Justin's Top Ten Values, it's easy to see how he would feel some affinity for the yoga teacher, who on the surface seemed the very embodiment of health.

But after just a few dates with her, Justin began feeling some dissonance. To his surprise, she wasn't nearly as committed to a healthy lifestyle as he assumed she would be, particularly with regard to her choices around what she ate and drank. Looking deeper, Justin saw that while "Healthy Lifestyle" was still one of his Top Twenty Values, it wasn't essential enough to make it to his Top Ten. As he honed in on the vibration he was hoping to achieve through all his healthy lifestyle choices, he saw that the values of "Purity" and "Simplicity" were actually more fundamental to what he was committed to. Evaluating the yoga teacher through this lens, Justin saw that they were actually far from being a match.

One month after breaking their relationship off and meditating daily on the qualities of purity and simplicity, Justin met Luna, who is his equal in every way. In fact, I bumped into the two of them recently, absolutely glowing as they happily meandered their way through the aisles of Whole Foods; their cart overflowing with organic delectables. It turns out "Healthy Lifestyle" is not an essential vibration, because it can mean different things to different people.

With regard to seeking a partner who shares "Healthy Lifestyle" as a core value, I have actually coached quite a few clients who were shocked and dejected when they discovered that the massage therapist, naturopath, or chiropractor they'd partnered with was committed to anything but. The point is, a person's title, position, or profession is not always an accurate barometer to use when assessing core compatibility. It's the vibrational essence you want to hone in on instead.

With these examples in mind, revisit your list of twenty through the lens of paring it down to the ten essential states of being you wish to live in. Remember that what you're ultimately going for is the vibrational frequency that you desire to cultivate, nourish, and attract into your life.

The third and final step in the values clarification process is to distill from your Top Ten Values list down to what I call your "Nonnegotiable Six." To do this, simply review your list of ten core values through the lens of the most important lessons life has taught you thus far, and use this hard-won wisdom as a way to further pare down and prioritize. This will allow you to discern the difference between the values you simply desire to surround yourself with, and those that are truly Nonnegotiable for you.

For example, as I reflect on the heartaches I've experienced in intimate relationships, in friendships, and in business alike, what emerges as a common theme is my childhood tendency to trust too freely, before trust had actually been earned. In the past, I prioritized Partnership, Intimacy, Security, Fun—and a host of other values—ahead of Trust. And then Life, in its abundant wisdom, showed me that Trust, for me, is priority number one. Simply from reflecting on your past heartaches, you can easily begin to discern your Nonnegotiable Six.

So, as you review your list of Top Ten Values, begin to overlay these with the toxic relationships you've been in or with the friendships or business deals that went sideways. What qualities within yourself do you wish you had had greater access to? What did those relationships teach you about what is truly important to you?

To make the cut from your Top Ten Values to your Nonnegotiable Six Values, ask yourself this: *What qualities has my past experience shown me that I simply must have in place? What qualities have I learned that I simply cannot live without?*

Here are my Nonnegotiable Six Values in order of importance:

1. *Trust*
2. *Family*
3. *Authenticity*
4. *Healthy Lifestyle*
5. *Freedom*
6. *Spirituality*

Once you've refined your personal values down to your essential, Nonnegotiable Six, I recommend thinking about, speaking about, journaling about, and meditating on these vibrations daily. One client I worked with even had hers printed and laminated and kept them in her wallet for ready access!

Of course, this values clarification process works best in advance—not after you've bought the house, married the guy, or moved cross country for the job. Ideally this is an inquiry we engage in within ourselves before we're faced with those kinds of big decisions.

Once you're clear about your Nonnegotiable Six, you will begin to see life through this filter, through your particular lens, and it will be a lot easier to say Hell Yes to those things that align with you and Hell No to those things that don't. But as nice as it is to do this inner work in advance, it's also true that every new moment is a potential turning point. It's never too late to mine whatever situation we're currently living for the clarity that it holds.

Remember that the process of defining your Nonnegotiable Six is very personal, and there are no right or wrong answers. Your work is to discover, then resonate in the frequency of energy that uplifts and inspires you. Other people may or may not understand this, and that's perfectly okay.

Don't try to explain yourself to people who are not on your wavelength. Don't spend a lot of your time and energy trying to pull them up to where you are. For one thing, focusing your attention on another person's experience above your own creates blind spots in your own self-awareness. And second, in trying to uplift them, you will likely end up meeting them in their vibrational set point, rather than raising them to yours. So instead, choose the vibrational tone of your life. Play that tone as often as you can. Enjoy those whom you are naturally and already grooving to at that same frequency. And bless those who are marching to the beat of a different drummer, and allow them to get on their way.

Finding Your Why

Your boundaries and values don't just reflect *what* you want, they lead you into the fruitful discovery of *why* you want it. The why that underlies each of your core values is the energetic essence of all that life has caused you to hold dear. When we connect to the why that underlies something we value and aspire toward, we can then understand what we hope will be available to us once we've integrated a particular quality. And unless we do this deeper investigation, we're likely to chase a particular set of circumstances rather than hone in directly on the core vibration we're really seeking.

Your why is the foundation that will be here to support you when life goes a bit sideways—which, by the way, it will. After all, we live in a diverse world which we have free will to navigate as we choose, so we are bound to find ourselves having turned down a path that looked good at the outset but is ultimately not aligned with our deeper needs and desires. Clarifying your values and then anchoring yourself to the deeper why that underlies them is a process of becoming intimate with yourself and then declaring who you truly are.

Armed with the information about what you value and why, you become like a lighthouse, standing tall and shining as bright as a beacon, vibrating your precise frequency. Your why is your sonar, and the call echoes out, reverberating with all who are energetically aligned with you. This signal is as unique as your signature or your DNA, and broadcasting it clearly and proudly is the key to attracting like-minded people and experiences into your life.

Here are six questions you can ask yourself to connect with the why that underlies each of your important values:

- What are my Nonnegotiable Six Values?
- Why do these values matter to me?

- In what ways do I hope these vibrations will shape my thoughts, beliefs, and behaviors?
- How do I believe I will feel on a day-to-day basis once these values are firmly anchored in my life?
- What do I stand to gain by honoring my truth and prioritizing my values?
- What do I stand to lose by not honoring my truth and prioritizing my values?

Your why is your calling. It is your conviction. It is your mission statement. It is a vision of your life and a blueprint of all you wish to accomplish while you are here. Think of it this way: Defining what you value and why you value it helps you to fashion a life that you love; a life that feels like home to you, and that nourishes you from the inside out.

Designing a Well-Loved Life

A well-loved life is made up of the small experiences you create for yourself every single day. Over time, these build momentum and lead you incrementally on track to create the kind of life you have always dreamed of.

I have been incredibly blessed to sit at the sides of a few dear friends as they prepared to make their transition out of this life. And although they had never met one another, each of them came to some of the same essential revelations in their final days. At some point, all of them expressed to me things they regretted about their journey here, and I was struck by how these regrets seemed to follow a common theme that goes something like this:

I wish I had taken more chances. I wish I hadn't allowed fear to dictate so many of my choices. I wish I had been bolder and more adventurous. I wish I had had the courage to walk away from the people and things that promised me safety, and to venture into the unknown that I felt my soul urging me toward. I wish I had dared to live a life that was true to myself. I wish I had followed my soul's calling, and I hadn't concerned myself so much with what others expected of me.

What this values conversation is about is supporting you in designing a life that feels good to YOU, and that is reflective of the kind of person you desire in your heart to be. It's about being able, at the end of this wild Earth ride, to look back in self-appreciation and pride at all the times you followed your heart and did what felt right to you, even if it meant taking the road less traveled. Never discount the benefit of even small choices that move you in the direction of what you love and value. Because while they may be so small as to be almost imperceptible at first, over time they add up. Until before you know it, the entire tone and fabric of your life has changed.

Meditation teachers often liken the process of meditation to that of dying a piece of white fabric. When you meditate, you withdraw your attention from the outer world of form and submerge your consciousness in the formless inner world of spirit. Then, at the end of your meditation period, you reemerge back into normal waking consciousness and go about your daily life, bringing a bit of the boundlessness of spirit with you.

The parallel is that each time you meditate it's like dipping a white piece of fabric into a vat of colored dye. When you pull it out of the dye, some of the color remains. You then hang the garment to dry—which is akin to focusing your attention again on the world of name and form—and some of the color naturally fades in the wind and the sun. But each time you submerge it, more and more of the color remains until eventually the garment becomes colorfast.

It's the same way with every choice you make that is in alignment with your why. These choices begin as small, imperceptible moves that may not seem to be altering your life trajectory at all, until one day you realize that you're standing firm in your truth and attracting people and experiences that reflect your new frequency. At that point, you no longer need to shout your preferences and boundaries from the rooftops. You no longer need to make anyone else wrong for the way they are choosing to live their lives. You simply recognize when your path and that of someone else simply doesn't align, and you continue choosing in the direction of your values and your why, easily and elegantly.

Your work is to care about, and be deliberate about, vibrating in alignment with your values. And to care about and be mindful of the moments when you are tempted to ignore or disregard them. Your values are like signposts that call your attention to the direction of your everyday choices. Eventually you will become sensitive enough to your own vibration—and the vibration of those around you—that you'll recognize ahead of time the paths that are in line with your best interest and those that are not. And, if and when you realize that you've strayed from your intended path, please do your best not to beat yourself up. Simply remind yourself of the vibration you're interested in cultivating in your life and as elegantly as you can, go about making a new decision.

Realize that the entire time you were living what you do not want, you were gaining greater clarity about what you do. The processes of "Uncovering Your Nonnegotiable Six Values" and "Finding Your Why" help you to focus in on your Yeses, and when you do, the Nos. have a way of taking care of themselves.

So, you no longer have to police the universe to make sure unsavory people do not make their way into your experience. You don't need to try to guard against unwanted vibrations. When and if you stumble into a relationship or situation that doesn't feel good, do your best to lie low, disengage, and return to your own center. Revisit the restorative practices we explored together in part two. Take really good care of yourself. Thank yourself for having received the guidance that something doesn't feel quite right—even if you received the guidance somewhat after the fact. Remember to breathe deeply and remind yourself that you always have the ability to make a new choice.

You need only to marinate on what you want, and place it at the center of your thoughts and actions. That which doesn't match the vibrational bandwidth you're living in will bounce off you, and in time, will no longer even show up on your radar, because you're now vibrating on a new frequency. This is the path to generating positive momentum toward all that you want. Not one decision we make in our lives should exclude this foundational piece.

CHAPTER 11

LIVING OFF THE MAP

If we juxtaposition the place where this book began—
from uncovering the blind spots, the back doors, within
our psyches that leave us susceptible to toxic relationships
and situations—to the place we now stand, one thing
becomes clear. The "maps" we turned to for guidance in
our earlier years, heavily influenced as they were by the
wounding events of our childhoods, were simply not
capable of leading us to the well-loved lives we now desire
to create.

As we've seen in the stories shared throughout this
book, the wounded parts of us create and then perpetuate
a certain narrative—a life script that we continue to repeat
until we're ready to acknowledge our blind spots and bring
loving attention to the places within our psyche that are
unhealed. This wounded narrative is self-perpetuating,
in that it only gives us access to people, situations, and
experiences that confirm what we already believe about
ourselves and the world, while filtering out everything
outside of that limited vibrational bandwidth. The scripts

authored by our wounded self tell us what we deserve and don't deserve, how much of our authentic self is acceptable to express, and what we must tolerate and sacrifice in order to be loved. And until we change this internal script, the conditions of our outer lives don't really change in any meaningful or lasting way.

This explains why the surface details of each of the abusive relationships we've experienced may have differed, but the underlying dynamics are eerily the same. It explains why we get fooled, time and time again, into believing that we're charting a new course for our lives, only to find ourselves once again falling into the same familiar patterns. We may think we're free to choose from the infinite number of experiences this life has to offer, but when we're living from the dictates of our wounded self, we only have access to the limited range of choices that fall within the scope of that outworn map.

And here it's important to acknowledge that these unconscious maps—God bless them—were created for one single purpose: To help us endure unstable, unpredictable, unsafe, or "or all-of-the-above" childhoods. And as a result, our childhood maps can only guide us down a very narrow path in life, along which our main objective is to survive, avoid further wounding, and seek from the outer world the right person or conditions we hope will bring us the sense of inner wholeness we've always felt was missing. In other words, our childhood maps—while well-intentioned—lead us into a world of hurt. Until we bring them into the light of awareness, our unconscious programming will continue to guide us into making the same automatic and reflexive choices, which is why we so often find ourselves living out the same familiar scenarios but with different people and in different places—a dynamic which I affectionately refer to as *Groundhog Day*. But right now, there is an entirely different life script available to you, one that is grounded in self-awareness and self-love.

By now, I hope that you are more keenly aware of the gaps in your own self-awareness, and the ways in which you were never healthily constellated within your family of origin. You're certainly more mindful of the beliefs and behaviors that make up your psyche's back door, and in that mindfulness are much better equipped to cherish the temple that is your body, your mind, and your soul. You are now ready to take a calculated detour from the map that guided your earlier years, and to live your life off the map, in a whole new frequency of vibration. *And* to get there, you will have to rely on a whole new set of navigational skills.

Fortunately, through the inner work you've done throughout this book, you have already begun to hone these important skills. You now know that the most important relationship in your life is your relationship with yourself, and you're making your wellbeing your first priority. You've re-established and strengthened your connection with your intuition and emotional guidance system. You've begun to rethink and restructure your life according to the unique values and desires that matter most to you, to prioritize your own interests, and to take a stand for both your Hell Yesses and your Hell Nos. And perhaps most importantly, you now understand that those who push your boundaries ultimately come bearing the priceless gift of helping you to become of more self-loving and self-aware. So the very good news is, when it comes to living a well-loved life, you already have within you everything you need to chart the course.

Throughout this book, we've sampled an extensive menu of rituals and practices all designed to help you remain true to yourself, and to re-center yourself when you feel you've gone astray from your own True North. And now I want to tell you that all of these practices will come as naturally to you as breathing in the presence of this one single commitment:

Making a commitment to feeling good is the key to living a well loved life that is unrecognizable from anything you've experienced before.

It may sound simplistic, but this one intention will guide you through any situation you find yourself in.

Feeling Good: Your Empowerment Compass

Feeling good—which means feeling at ease, at peace within yourself, and empowered in each moment to express who you are, authentically and unapologetically— is much more than just a fleeting emotion. It's a state of alignment between the physical, emotional, mental, and spiritual dimensions of your being, and it's also a state of alignment, harmony, and synch between you and the universe at large. Feeling good is one of the highest goals we can strive for, because if we hit this mark, we find that staying in tune with ourselves and listening to and honoring our own needs and desires are easy and natural outcomes.

To make a commitment to feeling good is to make a habit of noticing every time you begin to feel bad about something and to stop, breathe, and reconnect with what you really want in that particular situation and moment in time; with what will lighten your heart and bring you joy. In terms of how a commitment to feeling good shows up in your moment-by-moment self-talk, it might sound something like this:

> *It's okay for me to stay grounded in my own experience. It's okay for me to wait until I feel that I am mentally, emotionally, and energetically aligned before taking action. I am consciously choosing to make my own wellbeing my highest priority, and I give myself permission to disengage from anyone and anything that diminishes it.*

When you make a commitment to feeling good, you realize there are certain things you are simply not able to give your attention to, because doing so takes your vibration into an unwanted, not-good-feeling place. You may realize you need to step away from things like the neighborhood gossip and evening news, because you can't tune in to those information streams and simultaneously maintain your vibration. You may conclude that certain activities that once felt okay to you no longer do, as your tastes begin to shift and evolve. Your newfound sensitivity—to intuition and to the subtle fluctuations in your own thoughts, moods, and emotions—is a sword that cuts both ways. It can help you tune into your deeper desires, values, and callings, and it also makes you less tolerant of people and situations that don't align with those desires and values. And over time, you truly do develop the willingness to turn away from those people and activities that don't resonate with you, and turn toward those that do—even if this means spending more time in solitude or withdrawing from activities you formerly believed you "should" participate in.

Eventually, with enough practice, the commitment to feeling good becomes automatic and you'll find yourself naturally checking in with your inner world and staying in tune with even the slightest fluctuations in your energy field. Because I'm a mom, I have come to think of these regular inner check-ins as a process of taking our own temperature.

Taking Your Own Temperature

When someone you love is under the weather, you take their temperature as a way of monitoring their wellbeing. And the practice of taking your own temperature works in much the same way. It includes taking time out after an encounter to honestly assess whether it added to your life force energy and left you feeling energized and empowered, or whether it left you feeling more nervous, agitated, or depleted. So in practical terms, this means pausing after the meeting, the phone call, or the first date, and really inquiring into whether you feel better or worse as a result. And then allowing yourself to actually *feel* whatever emotions and sensations are present so you can receive the messages they're communicating to you. Again, with practice, you'll be able to take your own temperature on the spot, in real-time when an interaction is unfolding, and before you've made the choice to do something that isn't ultimately in your own best interest.

My client Cassie had been in a year-long relationship with her boyfriend Mike, whose values deviated pretty significantly from her own. Mike was an extrovert through and through. Nothing thrilled him more than flitting from one social encounter to the next, and he felt even more enlivened when he was the one hosting the affair and at the center of the action. Cassie, on the other hand, was naturally more introspective and introverted, and while she enjoyed people, experience had taught her that she needed time alone between social events to unwind and recoup her energy in order to show up at her best.

Over the months that I coached her, Cassie and I explored the disparity in hers and Mike's views, and came up with a list of temperature-taking strategies she could put in place to support her wellbeing. As she worked on implementing these practices, Cassie discovered that it was fairly easy to monitor her own temperature when she and Mike were spending time together alone, but became much more difficult when other people's intentions were added into the mix.

One weekend, the two flew to Mexico for a friend's destination wedding, and arrived a day later than most of the other guests. As soon as they got to the hotel, they heard loud laughter and shrieks in the distance. After checking in at the front desk, they walked by the pool and discovered that the wedding party and many of their friends had commandeered the area and were engaged in an animated game of "chicken." Mike was drawn to the action like a moth to a flame, but Cassie had been looking forward to unwinding for a bit in their hotel room before joining their friends for dinner. Despite the hot weather and long flight, the idea of getting into the pool was entirely unappealing to Cassie.

When they got up to their room to unpack, Mike announced that he was going down to join their friends, and insisted that it would be rude if Cassie didn't accompany him. Not wanting to be perceived as standoffish, Cassie reluctantly agreed. Ignoring her body's request for rest, she poured a drink, changed into her bathing suit, and she and Mike joined the others for a swim.

Within just a few minutes of being in the chlorinated water, Cassie's skin and throat began to burn, her eyes watered profusely, and she felt nauseous. She had succeeded in talking her mind out of its objections to being social when she didn't feel like it, but her body registered the discord. Unable to ignore her physical symptoms, Cassie explained to the others that she wasn't feeling well, and went alone back to their hotel room to shower and recover. Ironically, after ignoring her own "temperature" just minutes earlier, and saying yes when a commitment to feeling good would have mandated that she say no, Cassie developed a low-grade fever and ended up spending that night in bed.

Physical symptoms, like those Cassie manifested, often arise as our psyche's last-ditch effort to get our attention when we've overlooked its more subtle clues. I have seen this so many times over the years. One client spent months discounting her frequent urinary tract infections, along with the nagging feeling that her partner was having an affair. When her physical symptoms persisted, she finally scheduled an appointment with her doctor. To her surprise (but not really), the sexually transmitted diseases panel he'd ordered (just to be thorough) revealed that she'd contracted gonorrhea. She was able to dismiss the troubling thought that her boyfriend was cheating, but her body was keeping score.

Another client, who begrudgingly agreed to host a second Thanksgiving get together for his wife's family, developed acute gall bladder pain in the middle of dinner—his body clearly communicating that he had more on his plate, literally and figuratively, than he could comfortably digest.

These types of visceral reactions—like getting cold feet, having a sinking feeling in your stomach, or feeling a shiver down your spine—are easily explained away, but they're almost always a manifestation of some unacknowledged emotion. And when we don't receive the early, subtle whisper of negative emotions and uncomfortable sensations when they first arise, they can pretty quickly escalate into a scream.

Developing mindfulness is one of the best ways to maintain this degree of moment-to-moment self-awareness. One particularly useful technique is to practice something called "double-arrowed attention."

Using Double-Arrowed Attention

My friend Danielle recently introduced me to the work of one of her early spiritual teachers, Dr. Vasant Lad, the founder of The Ayurvedic Institute in Albuquerque, New Mexico. In addition to being a gifted healer, Dr. Lad is a wise and beloved Vedic philosopher who explains the ancient science of Ayurveda as an art in moment-to-moment living. In his book, *Textbook of Ayurveda*, he writes about the simple practice of what he calls, "double-arrowed attention." In practicing double-arrowed attention, we remain aware of both dimensions of life simultaneously— the outer world of people and circumstances, as well as the inner world of our ever-changing thoughts and feelings. So, while we're engaged in a conversation with someone, one arrow of our attention is pointed outward, toward the person who is speaking. But at the same time, another arrow of our attention remains pointed inward—toward ourselves, the witnessing awareness who is listening.

Maintaining this quality of double-arrowed attention is a way of taking our internal temperature on a moment-to-moment basis. It allows us to monitor the subtle fluctuations of our own thoughts and emotions, even as we're actively engaged with others. Yes, we're still able to take in all the information provided by our five senses, but as we do, we are simultaneously noticing and responding to the flow of our own energy. This practice reminds us to continually bring our witnessing awareness back to the inner landscape of our thoughts and emotions, and to prioritize the information we receive from within just as much, if not more, as the information we receive from others. And when something is said or done that causes our energy to jam up or to plummet, we receive this as a valid and important communication from our inner wisdom, and respond to it appropriately.

Without this degree of self-awareness, it's easy to lose ourselves in what's happening around us, or become so attuned to other people's experience that we neglect our own. Double-arrowed awareness enables us to take greater responsibility for our moment-to-moment wellbeing, but it has another important benefit as well. By actively listening to the messages that your inner being communicates to you through the medium of your thoughts, emotions, and physical sensations, you tap into a powerful, intelligent guiding force. I think of it like a Cosmic Gulf Stream, for it is highly capable of directing you away from the map created from childhood wounding and toward the life you desire.

Surfing the Cosmic Gulf Stream

When you give up the illusion that clinging to survival mode is actually a guarantee of safety and instead allow yourself to ride the waves of the unknown, your life will feel less forced and more effortless, and your desires will unfold in ways you can't presently imagine. And this is because the universe truly loves you. The universe is a highly responsive, friendly place where you are intimately known and each of your heartfelt desires is heard. The universe is constantly, incessantly, giving you impulses and signs that will lead you on the path toward your most brilliant, realized life.

A few years ago, while attending an event, I found myself seated next to the Denver Broncos' Most Valuable Player. I thought to myself, *What in the world will I find to talk about with this person?* Football is not exactly my forte. What happened next changed my life, and deepened my understanding of the Cosmic Gulf Stream profoundly.

On a hunch, I asked this young athlete to describe what it feels like when he is in the zone. The question itself seemed to create an access point to some deeper wisdom, and this beautiful man grew thoughtful and quiet. His brown eyes gleamed as he told me that when he's in the zone, all the training, the practice, and the mental focus that led up to the game disappear entirely. In those moments, his heart and his passion for the sport that he loves so deeply is all he's present to, and he intuitively knows where to position his body and what next steps to take. How magnificent to receive life-changing wisdom from an NFL football player at a luncheon!

What this young man was referring to is the magical place I call the Cosmic Gulf Stream, and you can get there in many different ways. A passion for something bigger than yourself will guide your way in. Any creative endeavor that you care deeply about will drop you in as well. Often, all it takes is a willingness to acknowledge that this state of consciousness exists, and we can transcend the limits of our fight-or-flight reactions and open up to a whole new range of possibilities.

When we're in this state of consciousness—the zone—life seems to guide us effortlessly. Meaningful, joyful moments that we couldn't plan if we tried unfold with very little trying on our part. Ironically, to magnetize the ease, the inner peace, the happiness, and the abundance we all desire, we have to drop the illusion that we are the ones who have to make it all happen, and surrender to life's flow.

Sometimes we surrender joyfully and willingly, like the NFL star I was seated next to that day. And sometimes it takes intense, disruptive, or even violent events to cause us to finally let go. Why? Because the universe will stop at nothing in its quest to reunite us with our inner truth, and oftentimes it takes some pretty dire circumstances to awaken us.

I heard a beautiful example of this degree of surrender from Jon Gabriel, whose work I was introduced to a few years ago. Jon, who spent his thirties and forties working on Wall Street, is now a best-selling author, speaker, and renowned authority in the arena of health and weight loss. The path that ultimately led Jon to find both his happiness and his life's work was definitely dramatic.

In the late 1990s, Jon was working eighty hours a week as a stockbroker—a career which afforded him a certain measure of success, but was stressful, unfulfilling, and soul-sucking in virtually every other way. In fact, his lifestyle was not only killing his spirit, it was threatening his very life. Each year he spent working on Wall Street he steadily gained weight, and by the early 2000s he was morbidly obese, weighing in at over 400 pounds. Because he made a good living, he had the means to try every weight loss approach under the sun, but none of them worked. In fact, the more he dieted, the more weight he gained.

Jon had long dreamed of moving to Western Australia, and even took the step of purchasing land there, but his career kept him so busy that it never seemed like the right time to follow this calling and make such a bold move. He and his wife also very much wanted a child, but after eighteen months of trying, still hadn't become pregnant.

On the morning of September 11, 2001, Jon was scheduled to travel from the New York area where he lived to attend a weight-loss seminar in San Francisco, but due to a rare miscommunication with his business partner at the time, he ended up missing his flight. That flight was United Airlines Flight 93 from Newark to San Francisco, which as every American over the age of twenty knows, was hijacked by terrorists who took the lives of all forty-four passengers aboard.

This near-death encounter was the wakeup call that Jon needed. The experience sprung him loose from his default map, which warned him to stay put and stay safe, and filled him with a determination to finally listen to his heart. Feeling that the universe had truly given him a second chance at life, he decided it was time to stop postponing his happiness and to start making his real dreams come true. He quit his job and booked two one-way flights to Western Australia. Two days later, his wife learned that they were pregnant—a long-awaited dream realized instantly.

Since making that courageous decision in the direction of his own happiness, Jon has lost over 220 pounds without dieting or surgery, and his body shows virtually no signs of ever having been overweight—a fact that astounds professionals in the medical community. Jon is now an accomplished author and speaker, and a respected authority in his field. Even more importantly, he's living a healthy, happy, and abundant life that is in harmony with his inner truth. And this is precisely what happens when we stop forcing ourselves to do what we think we should, and surrender to the Cosmic Gulf Stream. We tap directly into the source of infinite intelligence and wisdom where everything we want to know or create exists.

As Jon's journey so beautifully illustrates, each of us reaches our own internal breaking point when we can literally no longer follow the mandates of our childhood maps; when, in the poetic words of Anais Nin, "the day comes when the risk to remain tight in a bud was more painful than the risk it took to blossom." True to this quote, I've discovered that it's usually the most painful life experiences that open us up to finally being willing to take this trust fall, and put our faith in that which is unfamiliar.

Jon spent a decade tolerating his job on Wall Street, even though it was draining him of joy and literally taking years off his life. And then one day, his limited perception was blown wide open and he simply couldn't tolerate it anymore. And the same is true for all of us. Something pushes us outside the margins of the maps that once defined us, and we fall into a whole new way of life. We all have our own thresholds of just how much discomfort we're willing to take before we're finally ready to surrender to life's flow, and allow ourselves to go in the direction that our hearts have been guiding us.

Now, is there a certain amount of terror in trusting in the unknown? Absolutely! But there is an equal if not greater terror in remaining enslaved by the past—to what your childhood map tells you must do in order to survive, to be secure, to prove your worth, to please your parents, or to fit in with society. And there's no end to that kind of terror. It wears on us year in and year out, aging us and draining of us of life force.

I once coached a man—I'll call him Rob—who sought me out because he was in an unhappy job and an unhappy marriage to the same woman he'd dated ever since high school. During the course of our work together, we explored the origins of his childhood map, which told him that security and stability were to be prized above all other things. He had built his entire adult life around these values. He told me how he'd graduated college with an art degree, but when his then-girlfriend became pregnant, he accepted a job in her father's insurance company. And at the risk of once again revisiting the case of the frog in the boiling pot, this man had been growing more miserable with each passing year.

In our work together, as Rob began to imagine himself untethered from those stifling conditions, what emerged for him was his previously abandoned interest in art, along with a desire to explore alternative music and films—and, to his genuine surprise, a desire to explore men. Unfortunately, this rediscovery of passions that had long been repressed was too much for Rob to process, and he discontinued our coaching not long after.

Just recently, I ran into Rob at a local shopping mall and barely recognized him. Even though it had only been a few years, he looked as though he'd aged a decade. I asked him how he was doing, and he joylessly answered that he was still working in the same job, living in the same neighborhood, and married to the same woman. As I wished him well and walked away from the encounter, a chill ran down my spine. This man, I thought to myself, is tethering himself, day in and day out, to the enslavement of The Known. Fear of the unknown may initially feel like something we should avoid at all costs, but complacency, over time, is a far more dangerous threat.

The Untethered Mind

As we've seen, the conditioned mind reflexively, repetitively asks, *How will I survive?* But a mind free from the constraints of our childhood maps seeks out that which brings us peace and nourishes our soul—regardless of what that looks like. And the cosmic joke is that as we begin guiding our choices according to what feels good, authentic, easy, and nourishing, our survival needs have a way of taking care of themselves and we truly do move from just surviving to thriving.

When we're following the path toward our own inner peace, we automatically and naturally place ourselves in alignment with the universe at large. As our nervous system receives the message that we're attending to and caring for ourselves, we're gradually released from the grip of fight-or-flight. And because we're no longer chasing external sources of security and validation, we actually have energy—to invest in ourselves, to receive inspiration, and to create. We find ourselves more and more often in a state of stillness, equanimity, and receptivity. And in this state, we can easily hear the whispers of the universe.

Whenever we catch ourselves in a vibration of scarcity and survival, the real work is to stop and breathe. The work is to remember that survival mode might be a familiar frequency, but there are countless, higher, better-feeling wavelengths we could choose. One of the most reliable ways I've found to make this leap in consciousness is to ask myself, *What thought, perspective, or action would bring me peace right now? What would spark joy? How can I place myself into closer alignment with my authentic self?*

Consider this, please: your highest work is to be happy. And if you will make your happiness—in other words, your alignment—the sun that you revolve around, all the other details of your life will sort themselves out. This is because alignment and timing are synonymous. When you're in alignment, you easily receive the vibrational impulses that are constantly emanating from the Divine. When you're aligned, you're not in your head, trying to control events in order to ensure your survival. Instead, you're firmly situated within your own being and in tune with your own energy. And therefore you can easily respond to the changing currents of life, like a skilled sailor naturally adapting to the winds and the tides.

When we're in the flow of life, we can feel when we're in the right place at the right time. Equally important, we can feel when something is slightly amiss. The keys are remaining sensitive enough to our own energy and committed enough to our own happiness that we can make the necessary adjustments.

I can't begin to recount the number of synchronistic connections and near misses I've experienced in my own life. From every day, mundane events that seemed in the moment to be of no consequence at all, to the most profound and dramatic occurrences that literally changed my way of life. And what I have come to trust in the very core of my being is that there really are no accidents, because in every moment of every day, we are being Divinely guided.

The coffee spilled on your blouse that delays your departure time by a few minutes and results in a meaningful rendezvous that you wouldn't otherwise have had. The impulse to slow down or speed up in traffic that positions you perfectly to avoid a major crash. The missed flight, as in Jon Gabriel's case, that not only saves your life, but sets it on a whole new vibrational trajectory. These things are not accidents. They are guidance. And those of us who are practiced at going within and listening to our own signals of comfort and discomfort are uniquely equipped to benefit from this guidance.

In time, you'll stop beating yourself up for the unplanned delays or missed connections. You will no longer get on your soapbox and argue that life isn't working out for you. Instead, what you will come to realize is that the timing is always perfect, the universe is always looking out for you, and there is as much grace in the missed connection—in the so-called *mistake*—as there is in the perfectly timed opened door. You come to appreciate the missed connections and the meetings that left you with a resounding No, as much as you relish the encounters that ring with an immediate Yes. Over time, you truly come to know that everything unfolding in your life gifts you with vital information, and you trust yourself to navigate your course in the direction that feels best to you. And in making this shift, you invite even more ease and flow into your experience.

It really comes down to this: When we feel *good*, this is our indication that we have departed from the limited map of life cobbled together by our wounded inner child, and are actively creating our life based on our values and desires. When we're living off the map, we are self-aware, we listen to ourselves, we restore ourselves regularly, we trust in the unknown to guide us, and we interact with life as a friendly place, knowing that things are always working out for us.

When we are no longer automatically making choices from a fight, flight, flee, or fawn level of consciousness, we become far more sensitive and responsive to the nuance of each moment. We more clearly see a situation's potential pitfalls as well as its opportunities. The clues were right in front of us the whole time, but when we're centered in our authenticity and committed to feeling good, we are so much better at recognizing them. We're able to read the subtle signs that point us in new directions, and are prepared to go with the flow when the stream of life naturally leads us in a new direction.

CONCLUSION

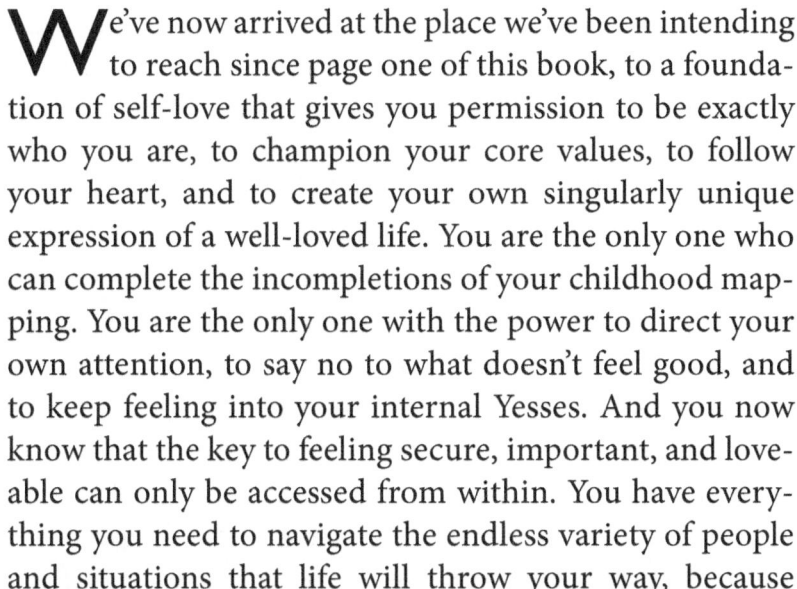

We've now arrived at the place we've been intending to reach since page one of this book, to a foundation of self-love that gives you permission to be exactly who you are, to champion your core values, to follow your heart, and to create your own singularly unique expression of a well-loved life. You are the only one who can complete the incompletions of your childhood mapping. You are the only one with the power to direct your own attention, to say no to what doesn't feel good, and to keep feeling into your internal Yesses. And you now know that the key to feeling secure, important, and loveable can only be accessed from within. You have everything you need to navigate the endless variety of people and situations that life will throw your way, because you can trust yourself to selectively sift from each one the aspects that resonate with your soul, and gracefully release the rest.

You now have a well-stocked tool kit of self-loving rituals that you can choose from, and with practice, you'll intuitively know which to call upon in which situation. Like a seasoned chef knows when a sauce needs a little lemon, a little salt, or a pinch of an herb, you will know when it's time to set a robust boundary and when it's time to retreat into yourself, to replenish your energies and regain clarity.

But perhaps most important of all, you have come to understand that the wounding events of your younger years were not without purpose or value, for they were instrumental in shaping you into the person you are today. After all, how could you know how good it feels to reconnect with your inner truth had you never forsaken or overridden that connection? How could you know the simple pleasures of inner balance, if you'd never allowed yourself to become swept up in chaos? You wouldn't know the profound relief of self-acceptance, unless you had known the exhaustion and futility of seeking approval from others. Your previous wounding—and the depth of wisdom you now possess as a result of it—was vital to the evolution of who you now are.

From the powerful inner realms of life, your soul has been calling you to go deep within, and the most painful experiences of your life have all been instrumental in your awakening. What's common is to ignore this deeper truth until circumstances become so dramatic that you are forced to listen. But whatever the experiences that brought you to this point, know that you will emerge from every dark night of the soul clearer, wiser, and determined to do whatever is necessary to preserve your connection with yourself.

Now, will you run up against people who don't listen to your needs or honor your requests? Most likely. After all, the intention of this book was never to teach you to build walls so thick as to isolate yourself from every potentially unwanted experience, but to increase your awareness of your personal preferences and empower you to respond to any transgression gracefully and appropriately.

You will hit bumps in the road, of course, but in doing so you will discover that now—unlike in your childhood and the relationships of your past—you are there to catch yourself, process the shock, and lovingly guide yourself back on course. After all, YOU are the foremost expert in your own wellbeing, and YOU are your most qualified advocate and valuable resource. Anytime you find yourself in a dead-end situation, circling the same loop over and over, you have the tools to care for yourself, to reprioritize your values, restore your nervous system, and recalibrate. Yes, the same non-serving choices still exist, but you're on a different frequency now, following the clues that lead you in the direction of your most authentic self-expression.

So when something shows up in your path that feels uncertain—be it a vague red flag or a flagrant NO— remember that this is not a condemnation of who you are, and it doesn't need to launch you into survival mode. You're not fighting for your survival anymore. You don't need to panic and throw any babies out with the bathwater. You always have an abundance of options. Within each situation there are an infinite number of variations and choices, and you have the ability to precisely curate your experience in order to achieve your desired outcome.

Recently I had a conversation with the very charming owner of a multi-media company about building a website to support the launch of this book. Everything about the meeting felt like a yes, and I eagerly took the next step of meeting with his website copywriter to describe my work and the intention of this book. But what transpired in the course of that conversation felt like the very opposite of a yes.

Instead of an easy flow of ideas and a mutual understanding of the energy I desired to provide for my website visitors, the conversation was forced and I even felt some pushback from her about the nature of the work I do. Initially I was disappointed: the direction I had chosen to go, which felt like a strong yes days earlier, now seemed to be going off the rails.

Then I remembered the advice I'm giving you now: that within every situation, person, and experience there are both positive and negative aspects. These are not in a moral sense of right and wrong but in the sense of what is beneficial and not so beneficial for us. And we can choose from within each situation the aspects that resonate, and simply let go of the ones that don't.

Every experience provides us with the exact building blocks we need to recreate it better than before. We just have to be willing to feel ourselves, reassess our position, and speak our truth. Sometimes this means making a subtle shift in a project or a relationship, and sometimes— as was the case with this website developer—it means walking away. The point is, as long as we're willing to look at our part in the creation and to integrate the wisdom that's being offered to us, we never walk away empty handed.

So, continue finding your own groove and enjoying the singularity of your experience. Continue reading the signs that present themselves in your path and continue choosing in the direction of your own happiness. Then, in your vibration of sovereignty and personal contentment, watch who comes to play with you.

RESOURCES

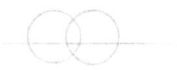

Domestic Violence
The National Coalition Against Domestic Violence. Trained advocates are available 24 hours a day, seven days a week, by phone or via live private chat.

(800) 799-SAFE (7233)
www.thehotline.org

Neo-Shamanic Breathwork
Neo-Shamanic Breathwork and Neo-Shamanic Shadow Work were developed by James Frazier. He has been leading Breathwork workshops and a busy personal growth coaching practice for almost four decades. James has developed a unique process that seeks to combine the best of Shamanic sensibilities with the tremendous insights of depth psychology, especially the Jungian and Neo-Jungian models.

James Frazier:
www.JamesFrazier.com

Managing Stress and Overwhelm
Managing stress, overwhelm and transforming procrastination.

Kristen Howe:
www.kristenhowe.com

Transformational Retreats
Adventure, growth, and connection through heart-led experiences.

Joe Hawley:
www.hartcollective.org

Whole Person Healing
Addressing the dis-ease at the body, mind and soul levels.
Reena Parikh, founder and spiritual director:

www.energetica.ca

Emotional Mental Detox
Designed to uninstall self-limiting beliefs, fear, painful memories and emotional triggers.

Suzanna Kennedy:
www.suzannakennedy.com

Childhood Trauma
Understanding the "fawn" survival response.

Pete Walker, MA, LMFT:
www.pete-walker.com

Reiki
Japanese form of energy healing.

The International Association of Reiki Professionals:
https://iarp.org

Neurolinguistic Programming
(NLP), a powerful methodology that helps shift limiting mindsets and release core patterns.

The Association for NLP:
https://anlp.org

The work of Dr. Michael Hall:
www.neurosemantics.com/michael-hall

Hypnotherapy
The American Association of Professional Hypnotherapists:
www.aaph.org

Counseling
One-on-one, couples, family, and group therapy addressing a wide variety of issues, including anxiety, depression, relationship issues, parenting, divorce, eating disorders, and substance abuse.

Dr. Sharon J. Strauss, PhD:
www.psychologytoday.com/us/therapists/sharon-j-strauss
-aspen-co/54224

Mediation

If you're drawn to meditation, here is one that I guide my clients to use daily. You can download it at www.Radically AuthenticYou.com/gift or scan the QR code below.

ACKNOWLEDGMENTS

First and foremost, I wish to express my gratitude to my Divine Team of Love, which inspired this book, and continues to offer meaningful guidance on how to live life, empowered and sovereign.

My heartfelt thanks and appreciation also go out to those who shared their stories and personal triumphs in reclaiming their sovereignty through the experience of toxic relationships.

And finally, my deepest gratitude to Danielle Dorman, who gave this book life and guided me along the path.

ABOUT THE AUTHOR

L isa Wilson has devoted the last twenty-five years of her life to the understanding and application of energy healing, and has studied everything from Shamanism and soul retrieval to rewiring outdated programs and limited beliefs. She has a full-time practice as a transformational coach, and is also a certified hypnotherapist, a practitioner of neuro-linguistic programming, a Reiki master, and a Unity Breathwork facilitator. Lisa has guided hundreds of women and men to reclaim their personal power, restore their physical, emotional, and psychic energies, re-establish their values and boundaries, and become spiritually centered in their own lives. You can visit Lisa online at www.RadicallyAuthenticYou.com.